ALASKA NATIVE CORPORATIONS:

SAKUUKTUGUT

"We are working incredibly hard"

The land, the money, the history of the Alaska Native Claims Settlement Act of 1971 and how Alaska Native people are writing an epic story in cultural and economic development.

— By —

Alexandra J. McClanahan

The CIRI Foundation is the recipient of proceeds from the sale of this book.

THE CIRI FOUNDATION

Anchorage

CIRI Photo

ISBN 0-938227-07-6

10 9 8 7 6 5 4 3 2 1

TABLE OF CONTENTS

Cover photo by Chris Arend: The CIRI Boardroom is featured in the cover photo. Artwork shown includes three sculptures by Kent Heindel, from left, whalebone Raven Mask Dancer, whalebone and jade Walrus Totem, and whalebone and walrus ivory Aleut Hunter. Mounted on the wall above are, at left, a traditional Siberian Yupik harpoon made of wood, ivory, baleen, walrus hide and sinew by Walton Irrigoo and an Aleut hunting spear set made of wood, ivory and sinew by Peter Lind.

FOREWORD

By Susan A. Anderson, M.Ed.
President and CEO, The CIRI Foundation

Alaskans need a basic primer to help them understand the Alaska Native Claims Settlement Act of 1971. Alaskans need a greater appreciation for the key role Alaska Native Corporations play in the state's economy. And Alaskans need to know that Alaska Natives made a conscious decision to create a new model based on what has become a new form of capitalism, rather than reservations.

Sakuuktugut, an Inupiaq word pronounced *suh-KOOK-to-ghut* and translated as "we are working incredibly hard," goes a long way toward answering this need. It would be impossible to publish a text that would answer all questions about the Act, known as ANCSA, but if nothing else, this book will encourage discussion about those questions and the many issues surrounding this grand experiment.

The CIRI Foundation's goal in publishing such works is to preserve and perpetuate the heritage of Alaska's indigenous peoples. ANCSA and the creation of Alaska Native Corporations is a milestone in the most recent history of Alaska Natives. We believe the ANCSA story can only be understood in a historical context, and to that end we have published this book with two columns. On the inside, you will find the general narrative, discussing the Act and issues surrounding it. On the outside, we have included a number of brief historical articles, first published in the *Anchorage Daily News*, as well as quotes and photographs. These "History Scrapbook" features provide context. They complement the text with historical information about people and events that have surrounded ANCSA and serve as an enhanced timeline.

Alaska Native Corporations play a key role in Alaska's economy, but they are only one part of the Alaska Native Community, which also includes non-profit organizations that provide key services, as well as tribal entities that preserve the birthright of Alaska Natives.

Just as no one book can tell the entire "ANCSA story," no one "voice" can speak authoritatively on all issues. In this book, Gary Harrison, an outspoken tribal advocate, discusses his view of ANCSA and why he disagrees with much of it. Offering a very different viewpoint is Carl Marrs, former CEO and president of Cook Inlet Region, Inc., who believes that ANCSA was an act of self-determination. Sheri Buretta, Chugach Alaska Corp. chairman, says that Alaska Native Corporations are the main vessel for Native people to compete in the marketplace. Trefon Angasan gives his views on subsistence, and Aaron Leggett gives us a glimpse of what young leaders are feeling. Whether you agree or disagree with any of these views, it's important to know where they stand.

The CIRI Foundation seeks to foster informed debate and discussion, so we include a number of different authors in this book, even though they don't all agree with each other.

As the president of The CIRI Foundation, I take the long view. I look toward the future: not the immediate future of the next five years, but the long-term view of the future that will be peopled by those who today are teenagers or younger. I hope that this book will be read by Alaskans, discussed throughout the Native Community and used in schools by Native and non-Native students alike. I hope that people who disagree with any of the viewpoints in this book will talk about what they believe would be better in the long-term for the Native Community. Should all Alaska Native Corporations add those born after the 1971 cutoff to their shareholder rolls, or, can young people's needs be taken care of through inheritance? How can the subsistence issue be resolved in Alaska? Should all business decisions be made by looking through a "cultural lens"? What can be done about the natural tension between a focus on the bottom line and the need for cultural sensitivity? As a Tlingit, I struggle with these questions on a near-daily basis. I don't know the answers, and I don't know any one person who has them all. But I do know that healthy debate and respectful discussion will take us in the direction of finding them.

We are children of the Alaskan landscape, whether we or our forebears came from Ketchikan or Kotzebue. In the end, we will be responsible for that landscape, the land of our ancestors. This book may help us better understand our history. I believe it will foster greater respect for the leaders of our past and our present. And I hope it will encourage every single one of us to see more clearly that our actions today decide the fate of our greatest resource, our people. It is our people, acting as stewards of the land and other resources we oversee that will move us forward. The decisions of our people surrounding the land and bounty from the land are what we need to focus on together so that our children, grandchildren, and those to come will benefit from the courageous and creative decisions made by those who crafted ANCSA in 1971.

Morris Thompson greets President Ford in this mid-1970s photo.

Tundra Times photo

PROLOGUE

Alaska Native Corporations are unique entities in Alaska's cultural and economic history and the United States as well. The corporations were created under an act of Congress that is an experiment on a grand scale in federal relations with indigenous people. The act was a conscious and dramatic departure from the treaties with Indians in the Lower 48 that led to the creation of reservations.

Since they were created as a result of the Alaska Native Claims Settlement Act of 1971, these corporations have gone through financial and political ups and downs on their way to becoming powerful economic engines in the Alaska economy. By the year 2003, however, 41 of the nearly 200 corporations had combined revenues of $2.9 billion.

The Alaska Native Claims Settlement Act, known as ANCSA, authorized the creation of 12 regional corporations within Alaska, along with more than 200 village corporations. The 13th Regional Corporation was formed four years later for Alaska Natives living outside the state. The shareholder base for The 13th Region includes Eskimo, Aleut, and all Indian groups from Alaska; however, these Natives were living in the Lower 48 during the passage of ANCSA. There are currently a total of 169 village corporations and four urban corporations (Juneau, Kenai, Kodiak and Sitka) operating in Alaska. These are the corporations remaining after a number of villages merged either into their region or with one another.

Business endeavors of the corporations run the gamut in Alaska from real estate and natural resource development to construction, tourism, and retail operations. Additionally, many of the corporations have invested in a wide range of businesses outside Alaska. Major lines of business in addition to construction and real estate development are oil field services and tourism. In the last several years, there has been a notable increase in the amount of work Alaska Native Corporations do for the federal government, both inside Alaska and in the Lower 48.

The corporations' importance and influence continue to grow at an exponential rate, giving them a powerful political voice in the state. At the same time, the corporations concern themselves with the social needs of Alaska Natives, as well as their economic well-being. They are key employers of both Natives and non-Natives in Alaska, and the role they play in funding and supporting charitable organizations cannot be overstated.

While Native corporations have become sophisticated businesses with leadership that is very much at home in the office and the boardroom, Native people retain close ties to the land and their traditions. Tim Towarak, Native leader from Nome, tells a story of Frank Degnan, one of the early leaders from Unalakleet, who fought for passage of the Alaska Native Claims Settlement Act. In one short anecdote, Towarak is able to deftly illustrate that Alaska Natives have had a difficult job in trying to explain their hopes and their dreams to people who have come to Alaska from a very long way away. Something as simple as food is not meant to be translated or explained or even understood. It is to be savored. And yet, if Native people seek to explain what it is their Alaska Native corporations are about, they likely need to get back to the basics, back to the heritage, back to their survival – and back to their food.

"A little story on Frank Degnan: I don't remember the date, but it was in the early '70s when Senator Ted Stevens brought some other senators to Nome to hold a public hearing on housing and other needs of Western Alaska. When it was his turn to testify, Frank elaborated about all of the different foods derived from the sea, one of which was 'gowk' (part of the skin of a walrus). This fascinated the senators, who were writing down his story, and they asked Frank how to spell 'gowk.'

"His response was: 'We don't spell it. We eat it!' "

For Jeanne . . .

*Danielle Larsen photo
courtesy CIRI*

The Alaska Native Claims Settlement Act of 1971 has been a backdrop to my life for 23 years. When I moved to Alaska in 1982, I could never have guessed that this monumental and unusual decision by the Congress of the United States, a decision made at the urging of Alaska Natives to create a new form of capitalism instead of Indian reservations, would be a theme that I would literally live and breathe nearly every single day of my life. And yet, that is exactly what has happened.

The act, known as ANCSA, has colored my family life, it has shaped many of my friendships, it has forced me to work at being a better writer, it is intertwined in my relationship with my Inupiaq daughter and in a strange and odd way, it has led me back home. ANCSA is in my heart.

The *Anchorage Times* hired me in March 1982 to cover federal agencies in Alaska, and this was a very broad beat that encompassed the entire federal bureaucracy in the state, including the military. It just so happened that when I arrived, however, a debate was raging over a ballot initiative that would have taken away the subsistence preference in the state's fish and game laws in times of shortage. This was an issue of vital importance to Alaska Natives, but no one on the staff had the time or the inclination to cover the issue, so I was designated.

Over time, I also was designated to cover Native corporations because at that time in the state's history the federal government and Alaska Natives were still inextricably linked in the minds of many people. I became fascinated with these unique business entities and wanted to learn as much about them as possible. Many of the Native leaders at the helm of these corporations were among the most ardent supporters of subsistence and were working hard to make sure that the ballot initiative failed. As I became acquainted with them, I developed tremendous admiration and respect for them and all that they worked so hard to achieve. I can't say I was exactly a neutral reporter on the subsistence issue that year, but more than effecting political change through writing on the subject, I feel I probably was someone on the crest of a wave, simply carried along with it as it flowed through Alaska and eventually resulted in the failure of the ballot initiative, as well as the election of the pro-subsistence gubernatorial candidate in that election, Bill Sheffield.

I had moved to Alaska from Nebraska. In Nebraska I had worked my way up through several newspapers in the state, culminating in my work for the *Omaha World-Herald*, as a legislative reporter, specializing in agricultural and water resources issues in a state where water is the lifeblood that fuels farming and ranching, as well. It was an honor to work for the state's largest newspaper, and there was a huge responsibility that went with writing about a resource that ran through people, igniting their passions as well as their livelihoods.

City people in Nebraska often wanted to preserve and protect the state's underground water resources, while many farmers and ranchers were deeply offended that outsiders were trying to control them and their use of the resource that meant the difference between profit and loss, and more importantly the difference between being able to make a living and remain on the land of one's grandparents or not. Having grown up in a small rural community in northeastern Nebraska, my heart often leaned toward those engaged in agriculture. At the same time, it was becoming clear that mining water that had accumulated underground over thousands of years, as well as pouring huge amounts of fertilizers and pesticides on the farm ground likely had serious implications for the future of the underlying water resources.

What I witnessed growing up and later working as a journalist in Nebraska was the very deep and powerful relationship all the people had with the land – the landscape – of Nebraska. This relationship was com-

In the end, it always has been the land, it always is the land, and it always will be the land.

plex and even confusing at times, and it created alliances and divisions. Often, it had less to do with one's intellect than one's soul.

The first time I was sent to cover hearings before the Alaska Board of Game, where translators were used by some of the Yup'ik people offering testimony, I realized that many Alaskans' feelings about their land and their relationship to the landscape were every bit as deep. Rural people – mostly Alaska Natives – wanted and needed to be able to harvest resources from the land. Their urban neighbors often didn't understand their reliance on subsistence resources or they were frustrated and angry that use of a resource might be based on race and not freely available to all. Many city dwellers were completely unaware that subsistence is not simply to sustain the bodies, but also the traditions, the cultures, the souls. And it was this polarization that reminded me of my work in Nebraska. I recognized that people were often pitted against each other as a result of ignorance as much as any particular viewpoint.

Within a few years of my arrival in Alaska, I was hired for a grant-funded project associated with CIRI, one of the more financially successful Native corporations, to write an Alaska Native Elders' oral history book featuring 23 Elders from many regions of Alaska. As a result of that work, I was privileged to be given a glimpse into the lives of Native people representing all the major Native cultures in the state who willingly shared priceless information about their lives and their cultures with me and by extension with Alaskans who read the book, *Our Stories, Our Lives*. Many of the Elders talked about ANCSA and its impacts. The book itself stemmed indirectly from ANCSA because the foundation that obtained grants for the book, The CIRI Foundation, would not have existed had it not been for CIRI's financial success.

By 1986, the board of directors of the *Tundra Times*, asked me to become the president and publisher of the only statewide Native newspaper, founded in 1962 by the revered Inupiaq Native leader Howard Rock. At the time, I didn't understand that it was facing financial ruin with debts that had mounted to more than an entire year's revenues. In fact, the

Internal Revenue Service had seized the newspaper's bank accounts and was ready to close its doors. Although it required what sometimes felt like superhuman effort on the part of each of us on the tiny staff, we brought the paper back from the brink and became a forum for Native people to express their concerns.

We were able to focus much needed light on issues important to the Native community at the time, issues such as sobriety. We published editorials and articles highlighting key leaders in the Native community who had the courage to come forward and talk about their problems with alcohol and the devastation it had caused in their lives. Although we were always struggling to bring in enough revenue to cover our expenses, we swallowed hard and decided we could no longer run any liquor advertisements. Prior to that, each of us on the staff felt sick when we ran the full-page ad for "the traveler," a plastic bottle of whiskey that was preferred by bootleggers for its indestructibility. We were able to make this commitment in part as a result of a pledge by NANA Regional Corp. to assist in helping us make up the lost revenue.

Some of the other issues were the impacts of the *Exxon Valdez* disaster on subsistence resources, as well as a detailed look at the bingo industry in Alaska. We even undertook a major investigation into abuses arising from the fact that state law required bodies to be sent out of rural areas for autopsies in cases in which deaths were unattended by physicians. There were cases where miscommunication between bereaved families and funeral homes that held the bodies, sometimes for months at a time, led to agonizingly frustrating situations. Funding by Native corporations made all of our work possible, especially during our first most tenuous year when Arctic Slope Regional Corp., the Barrow-based Native regional corporation, stepped up to the plate and provided us with a significant source of much needed operating funds.

I stayed at the *Tundra Times* until early 1991. The year 1991 was something I had heard about, written about and studied for a number of years. The Native community struggled to come to terms with the fact that

Publisher refuses liquor ads

Native group picks up paper's lost revenue

The Tundra Times, a weekly newspaper whose readers are primarily rural Alaska Natives, stopped running liquor advertisements as of Feb. 1, the publisher said Monday.

A.J. McClanahan, who also is the editor, said she dumped the ads after NANA Regional Corp., an Native corporation in Western Alaska, offered to cover the loss of what is **McClanahan** expected to be about $4,400 annually in ad revenue. Total annual revenues at the Tundra Times are about $60,000.

"I'm extremely relieved that we can finally practice what we've been preaching."

She said the newspaper, with a circulation of about 4,000, has carried numerous editorials in the past few years pointing out and decrying the problems caused by alcohol abuse in Native villages.

NANA, which is headed by Sen. Willie Hensley, D-Kotzebue, "suggested the idea of helping us" by paying for the loss of liquor ad revenue, McClanahan said. Hensley is also a board member of the Tundra Times.

The paper's decision "is just a small step, but we've got to keep plugging away," Hensley said Monday.

Calling the decision a "symbolic gesture," Hensley said it came after readers questioned how the paper could take a position against alcohol abuse and carry liquor advertisements.

The *Tundra Times*' decision about alcohol ads draw coverage by the *Anchorage Daily News* on February 9, 1988.

CIRI Photo

"Like 1991. How many of the kids are going to hold their stock? Not very many. After 1991, I'd like somebody to tell me – and I don't care who it is – how many Indians are going to own land after 1991?"

— *Fred T. Bismark Sr., Tyonek, 1985*

ANCSA originally called for an end to restrictions on the sale of Native corporation stock 20 years after its 1971 passage. My husband and Julie Kitka, now the president of the Alaska Federation of Natives, and others were instrumental in crafting amendments to ANCSA to deal with that situation. In other words, without major amendments, the racially based ownership of Native corporations could have ended in 1991. It was a pivotal year for Alaska Natives. The "1991" amendments Congress approved were a radical shift for the act, because they ensured forever that Native corporations could remain Native for as long as the shareholders saw fit. And, of course, 1991 became the most important year of my life as I became a mother for the first and only time.

In February 1991, my husband, John Shively, and I adopted an Inupiaq baby girl when she was six days old. Her birth mother is a relative of Willie Hensley's. My husband had known Willie since his earliest days after arriving in Alaska as a VISTA volunteer in 1965, and he had worked closely with him during the years they both worked for NANA Regional Corp. I knew Willie from my work at the *Anchorage Times*, and he served as chairman of the *Tundra Times* board of directors during my tenure there. As a result of amendments to ANCSA, our daughter became a shareholder of NANA, which is one of three Native regional corporations that have added Native descendants born after 1971 as shareholders.

Carl Marrs, then-CIRI President & CEO, hired me as the CIRI Historian in 1998, and my charge was to document and explain ANCSA, gathering information and history, and all the while producing popular articles and books as opposed to scholarly works. Carl framed the job by saying he was specifically interested in learning about how Alaska Native people felt about ANCSA and how it had affected their lives. He said he wanted to know how Elders, Native leaders and young people felt about the act. Any discussion of ANCSA always led me in the direction of the importance of the land to the Native people, and eventually I began to question my own feelings about land and my own relationship to the landscape. I have always been struck by the beauty and grandeur of Alaska, and I will never stop marveling at the special quality of light at the end of each winter day. The only place in Alaska where I have truly felt at home, however, has been in Kotzebue, where the lack of trees and the rolling hills, stretching on for miles into a windswept forever, look a lot like the prairies where I grew up.

Over the years, I had made half-hearted attempts to obtain land in the Midwest, and at the same time, my work on ANCSA forced me to think hard about what it means to belong somewhere, really belong in the sense of having your heart sink right down into the soil. I continued with other oral history interviews with Alaska Natives of all ages, and as I listened to people tell their stories, again and again, it was the land that held their hearts.

In the spring of 2002, I found an acreage for sale in Antelope County, Nebraska, where I grew up. From the moment I saw the photograph of the rows and rows of trees in the two shelterbelts on the northern and western borders of the property, I knew where my heart belonged. To honor the people who are responsible for paying my salary, I chose the name Sht'uh Farm, a Dena'ina word provided by Professor Alan Boraas, which means "my special place" or "my home." Even though the name connotes a particular real estate transaction and ownership recognized in Western terms, in reality it feels more like this rundown little farm has been entrusted to my temporary care so that someone will take steps to protect its soil from the ever-present wind and to rehabilitate and preserve the house and barn.

In the fall of 2003, I became part of a team that began work on the development of a permanent exhibit at the Anchorage Museum of History and Art that focused on explaining ANCSA to the general public in clear and simple terms. My mother, Jeanne McClanahan, died in May 2004 during the development of that exhibit not long after she turned 85. Her death forced me to slow down, step back and think hard about the legacy one leaves behind.

Throughout my work at CIRI, I've been struck by the legacy that will be left by Carl Marrs. One of the most significant aspects of his legacy will be his efforts to shed light on the impacts of the Alaska Native Claims

> *"And to me, that is the one shining ray through ANCSA that gives me hope for the future. That deep down, Native people– instinctively, intuitively, culturally– understand the meaning of that land. Even as the corporations and the rest of the world look at it very differently. We could have sold it all and been very wealthy."*
>
> *— Byron Mallott, 1998*

Settlement Act. It entails honoring many diverse cultures and traditions, celebrating men and women who put their lives on hold for years at a time to make ANCSA work for Native people, and attempting to figure out exactly how capitalism is being molded and shaped by Alaska Natives.

While it has become fashionable to question the capitalistic system, my guiding light in regard to better understanding this system has been Hernando de Soto, who wrote in *The Mystery of Capital* that capitalism "is the only game in town. It is the only system we know that provides us with the tools required to create massive surplus value."

Tlingit leader Byron Mallott, who lobbied for ANCSA, served for years as the president of Sealaska Corp., the largest Native regional corporation, and later led a foundation focused on bettering the lives of all Alaska Natives, is cognizant of de Soto's point about capitalism being the only game in town. He says: "And yet, in my reading of history no racial minority will ever survive for long in a capitalistic society without having economic power or at least an economic ability to survive. And ANCSA gives us that. . ."

He's right. ANCSA has created powerful economic engines that have a significant impact on the entire Alaska economy. For the last several years the Association of ANCSA Regional Corporation Presidents/CEOs has published a report that documents the impact Native corporations have on Alaska. Michael J. Burns, former bank president, had this to say about the corporations in the first report: "They absolutely control the economic destiny of this state."

This book documents some of those impacts, as well as some of the differences between Native corporations and their more traditional Western counterparts. The Inupiaq word *sakuuktugut*, which means "we are working incredibly hard," shows at the outset that this is a story of hard work. It is a story of people examining their beliefs and their passions and crafting them into a tangible legal structure that is a living document that has been and will be amended many times. Quite simply, the story of ANCSA is indeed an epic story. And it is a story with many questions:

What is the history behind the sharing provision of ANCSA that took Native leaders 10 years to interpret? Why would a corporation be required to share some of its resource revenues with other corporations? What is the relationship of Native corporations to tribes in Alaska? Why does almost any discussion of Native issues in Alaska lead to a discussion of subsistence and its importance?

In the end, it always has been the land, it always is the land, and it always will be the land. I turn to Willie Hensley, whose 1980 speech on this subject is reprinted in this book:

> Basically, we did not fight for the land because it represented capital, or because it represented money, or because it represented business opportunities. We fought for the land because it represents the spirit of our people. It represents your tribes and it represents your ancestors and it represents that intimate knowledge of the land that your people grew up on for ten thousand years. And when we fought for the land, we really were fighting for survival – not economic survival, or political survival, but survival as a people with an identity – people with a culture. The land is the spirit of our people. It is the home of the spirits of our ancestors.

The stakes are as high as they come. My daughter's life will be grounded in the landscape, the landscape of Alaska and Nebraska. If she understands ANCSA, if all of those other Alaska Natives born after are able to seize the reins of their Native corporations and at the same time participate in their tribal communities, if they are able to take pride in their Nativeness, their cultures, their languages and their traditions, recognizing how deep their roots are to their own landscape, they will find ways to carve their names into the ground that holds their hearts. In the end, the land is the repository for the stories. The landscape nourishes our spirits because it is through our stories that we celebrate what it means to make

Gathering for the Oct. 27, 2004, opening of the permanent ANCSA Exhibit at the Anchorage Museum of History and Art were, from left, Elizabeth and James Hensley, Natasha Hensley Shively, Alexandra J. McClanahan and Willie Hensley.

CIRI photo

mistakes, pick ourselves up and reach for success. It is through our stories that we define what it means to be human, and these stories must be placed in the context of place to be truly meaningful.

For the young Dena'ina seeking to understand their culture, it's important to know the defining battle of the relationship between the Russians and the Dena'ina took place at Old Kenai. For any of us who want to better understand our heritage, it's important to know that our grandparents are buried there in those graves – directly north of that cabin. And for a child who seeks to come to terms with the loss of the most important person in his or her life, it's important to remember that Mother died here in this room. All of these are links in a chain that connect us to the land. The degree of their importance is determined by the spiritual connection that is always there, whether we recognize it or not.

—*Alexandra J. McClanahan*

1. AN EPIC STORY

Alaska Natives are writing an epic story in economic development. They are succeeding in their business endeavors by Western standards and their own, as well. Their ownership of vast tracts of land in Alaska is a powerful tool being used by Alaska Natives to create a new form of capitalism.

Nick Gray's last public appearance was a riveting experience still remembered today as a life-changing moment by some of those who were on hand October 19, 1966, to hear him.

The Seward Peninsula Eskimo – born November 26, 1900, in Council City – was the son of David Gray, a Russian Jew, and Mary Kegugnuk, an Inupiaq Eskimo.

His early experiences with discrimination made a lasting mark on him. When he was six years old, his father sent him to the Territorial School in Nome. It didn't matter that Gray's father served on the school board. Gray was turned away and told since he was Native he had to go to the Bureau of Indian Affairs School.

Sophie Chase and her husband Allan, who served on the CIRI Board of Directors for many years, were instrumental in helping Gray organize Alaska Natives in Anchorage. They met Gray after Sophie spotted an ad in the newspaper for a meeting of Alaska Natives at the Solarium of the Alaska Native Hospital in the early 1960s. When the Chases showed up for the meeting, they were the only two there in addition to Gray, who had

Native rights advocate Nick Gray died in 1966 not long after he gave a speech urging Alaska Native unity.
Wally Powers photo

"We want to be able to look at any man anywhere in the world and say, 'I am as good a man as you are.'"

— Nick Gray, 1966

placed the ad. When that happened a second time at the next meeting, both Sophie and Allan Chase visited their friends and relatives and urged them to come to Gray's meeting.

Sophie Chase said it was Gray's message that he wanted to "elevate our people" that grabbed their attention. She said Gray was remarkably advanced in his thinking for the time in Alaska's history.

Gray, a plain-spoken man who rarely wore a suit and tie, referred to the discrimination he experienced in his earlier years when he spoke for the last time in 1966:

"I came back to Alaska in 1923 after having graduated from school in California, and I saw a very distressful situation in Nome. Signs over the restaurants: We cater to the whites only. Even the bootleg joints had signs: We cater to the whites only."

In his speech, Gray said he decided then and there that he would be the person who would fight such injustices. But when he broached the subject with his father, he was told:

" 'Look, son, your people are scattered over the biggest land masses in Alaska, and they have no communication. The people here in Nome talk a different dialect than the people do in Kotzebue. The people in Kotzebue talk a different dialect than they do in Cape Lisburne. The people in Cape Lisburne talk different than they do in Point Hope. How are you going to communicate?

" '. . .You are dealing with the poorest people on earth. They have no money. How are you going to live?' "

Gray said his father's comments took the wind out of his sails. He then asked his mother what she thought.

"So my mother said, 'Yes, this is my country. I am shoved aside. I am tossed aside. There are restaurants I can't go to. There are laundries I can't take my laundry to, and believe me, I am not proud of my country. Something should be done, and

I am glad that you feel that you should do it.

" 'But, my dear son, remember this. You won't even get thanks.' "

Gray said he was so discouraged by their responses that he waited decades before he took up the banner. He was in his 60's by the time he began urging Natives throughout Alaska to organize and fight for their rights. And he was within days of dying when he found himself at that historic first statewide gathering of Alaska Natives in Anchorage in 1966. It was there that he spoke, issuing a challenge to each person attending:

"A time has come when we, as men – citizens – are ready to assume responsibilities that go with citizenship as well as the benefits. We want to be able to look at any man anywhere in the world and say, 'I am as good a man as you are.' "

Gray was far from being the first Alaska Native who urged Natives to work together to fight for Native rights. Many others had come before him and made great strides.

What was lacking in the earlier efforts, however, was a unified statewide organization bringing together Alaska's Eskimos, Indians and Aleuts, to name only the three main groupings of the many Alaska Native tribes and groups. And while no one person can be credited with the formation of the Alaska Federation of Natives, Gray certainly deserves mention as one of those who provided an impetus.

Anatoly Lekanof, who helped organize Cook Inlet Native Association, the first Native organization in Anchorage, burst into tears in an interview in the winter of 1999 when he recalled that he was with Gray shortly before he died on November 3, 1966.

"I cut his hair the day before he died. That's how much I knew Nick Gray. He was a dying patient at the old Native Medical Center. I don't know what from. . .And I said, 'Nick, you

U.S. Sen. Ted Stevens is shown with President Richard M. Nixon, who signed the Alaska Native Claims Settlement Act, in this 1971 photo.

Tundra Times photo

19

June 16, 1900, epidemic unleashes unparalleled despair

The influenza epidemic that eventually would become known as the "Great Sickness" began on St. Paul in the Pribilofs on June 16, 1900. Although possibly less well known than the devastating worldwide flu epidemic during World War I, the 1900 flu wiped out half of more of the residents of some Alaska villages, according to Robert J. Wolfe.

Wolfe discussed the impact of the epidemic in his 1982 paper, "Alaska's Great Sickness, 1900: An Epidemic of Measles and Influenza in A Virgin Soil Population." Robert Fortuine, author of the 1989 book *Chills and Fever*, said that the wave of illness that went through Alaska in 1900 can be compared only to an earlier smallpox outbreak.

"The smallpox epidemic of 1835-1840 and the influenza-measles epidemic of 1900 are both examples of historical events in Alaska that caused

Beds are ready for patients in this turn-of-the-century photo of the Flat Hospital, located in the Interior near Iditarod.
Anchorage Museum of History and Art photo

death, social disintegration, abandonment of traditional homes and despair on a scale unparalleled by anything but a major war," Fortuine wrote. "Never would the survivors of such overwhelming personal and collective tragedy be quite the same again."

Although it's difficult to pinpoint exactly where

could use a haircut. If you would trust me as a barber, I'd cut your hair.' "

Lekanof, like many others, would like to see Gray recognized for his achievements: ". . .if it wasn't for Nick Gray, the land claim issue would never have been."

Alaska's economy and history continue to be dramatically affected by ground-breaking legislation signed by President Nixon on December 18, 1971. The Alaska Native Claims Settlement Act was a profound change in U.S. policy when it was passed, and today it is a living document that has been dramatically changed in its more than 30 years of life.

Byron Mallott, former President & CEO of the First Alaskans Institute, has said that the experience of Native corporations created under the Alaska Native Claims Settlement Act, known as ANCSA, is an "epic story benefiting Alaska and all of its people."

Today, it is very difficult to imagine Alaska's economic and social landscape before ANCSA. That is due in part to the fact that passage of the act was a very positive step, and one that was a dramatic shift from decades of discrimination and policies seemingly designed to break the spirit of Alaska's First Peoples.

By the time non-Natives began arriving in Alaska, indigenous civilizations were spread across Alaska's vast reaches. Their cultures reached back for thousands of years. The first people to feel the effects of contact with the outside world were Alutiiqs, Athabascans, Tlingits and the Aleuts. The effect of the invading Russians on the Aleuts beginning in the mid-1700s was devastating. For most of the rest of the people living in Alaska, contact was relatively limited until after Alaska's purchase from Russia by the United States. Through the decades after Alaska's purchase in 1867, however, non-Natives pressed into Alaska's most remote regions, increasing pressure on vital subsistence resources and putting greater numbers of people over the years at greater risk of not having enough food.

Adding even more stress to the indigenous populations, successive waves of disease ranging from smallpox to influenza to tuberculosis wiped out thousands of people, and in some cases entire communities. These began with first contact and continued on through the 1900s.

One of the single worst blows came with an epidemic of measles and pneumonia in 1900, which is referred to as the "Great Sickness" by Native survivors. This was followed by yet another wave of death with the world-wide flu epidemic of 1918-19.

Western policies added another dimension to the difficulties. Both the missionaries and the federal education system for Natives had encouraged people, many of whom had traversed the wide, open spaces as nomadic bands, to settle into permanent enclaves. Although many of these villages were traditional gathering places, remaining in one place throughout the year made it much more difficult to obtain the life-sustaining fish and game food sources.

In 1924, Congress made citizens of all American Indians, including Alaska Natives. In the same year, Tlingit attorney William L. Paul became the first Alaska Native elected to serve in the Territorial Legislature. Paul and other Southeastern Alaska Natives eventually picked up the banner of Alaska Native land claims.

In his speech to the Alaska Native Brotherhood in 1977, Native rights champion Roy Peratrovich noted that it was during the Alaska Native Brotherhood-Alaska Native Sisterhood conventions of the 1920s that land claims were brought to the attention of Alaska Natives in Southeast Alaska. And they achieved at least a modicum of success.

In 1935, Congress passed a special act allowing the Tlingit and Haida Indians to bring suit on their claims against the United States for the lands taken from them. They then spent decades pursuing a lawsuit against the United States that stemmed from the 1907 appropriation of millions of acres of land in Southeast for the Tongass National Forest, which is today encompasses 17 million acres and is the nation's largest national forest.

In spite of such a glimmer of hope, there were few improvements in the

such illnesses begin, Wolfe's research indicated that the 1900 flu epidemic began June 16 on St. Paul, just days after the arrival of a North American Company steamship. At that point, almost all of the Aleut residents were affected. The Great Sickness appeared in St. Michael and the Seward Peninsula in late June, according to Wolfe, and eventually hit Eskimo and Indian communities along the Yukon and Kuskowkim rivers the hardest.

Fortuine said that what made the 1900 epidemic different from others was the fact that influenza and measles struck with "lightning force and within days whole villages were sick or dying." Wolfe, however, noted that despite the widespread devastation, Native people displayed impressive resilience. "Although relatively ineffective in managing the acute onslaught of infectious diseases, the Eskimos and Indians displayed a remarkably rapid social and economic recovery following the epidemic," he said.

- June 16, 2002

A female nurse stands outside the Flat Hospital in this turn of the century photo.
Anchorage Museum of History and Art photo

Frank Degnan, Unalit/Yupik leader from Unalakleet, helped form the Alaska Federation of Natives and served on its first board of directors.

Frances Degnan photo

July 7, 1901 – Birth of Frank Auvnue Degnan

Alaska Native leader Frank Auvnue Degnan was born July 7, 1901, in St. Michael. He was the only living child of Apok (Martha Annie Apok Degnan) and Francis Gerald Degnan. Degnan's Inuit name Auvnue means "cottonwood bark."

Degnan's life is chronicled in his daughter Frances Ann Degnan's 1999 book, "Under the Arctic Sun: The Life and Times of Frank and Ada Degnan." In it, Frances Degnan notes that Degnan's grandfather Auvnue was the last of the truly Unalit chiefs, whose life spanned the end of the Russian era in Alaska and ushered in the new era of American intrusion into Northwest Alaska.

Frank Degnan's family moved to Unalakleet when he was a child. His parents were close friends with the parents of Ada Johnsson, who eventually became his wife on June 26, 1934. The couple had 10 children.

Degnan held a number of local leadership positions in the village and also later served as the

social standing of Alaska Natives. When Roy Peratrovich and his wife Elizabeth moved in 1941 to Juneau, Alaska's capital city, they were stunned to find signs in front of businesses stating "We cater to White Trade only." In another place, they saw "No Natives Allowed," and "No Dogs or Indians Allowed." The Peratroviches sought help from then-Territorial Governor Ernest Gruening, who did what he could as far as asking individual proprietors to remove such signs. The Peratroviches realized that they needed to seek legislation to correct the situation, so they helped develop the Anti-Discrimination bill that was introduced in the Territorial Legislature during the 1943 session and was narrowly defeated that year.

Racism was blatant in many parts of Alaska in Territorial Days as shown in this 1908 photo of Juneau's Front Street.

Alaska State Library photo

The bill was finally passed in 1945, but not before vocal opposition from several senators, including personal attacks on the Peratroviches. An account of the exchange between Elizabeth Peratrovich and one of the senators is included in the book, *Haa Kusteeyi' Our Culture, Tlingit Life Stories.* According to the book, Sen. Allen Shattuck argued that the races should be kept farther apart, saying, "Who are these people, barely out of savagery, who want to associate with us whites with 5,000 years of recorded civilization behind us?"

Elizabeth Peratrovich responded: "I would not have expected that I, who am barely out of savagery, would have to remind gentlemen with 5,000 years of recorded civilization behind them of our Bill of Rights. When my husband and I came to Juneau and sought a home in a nice neighborhood where our children could play happily with our neighbor's children, we found such a house and arranged to lease it. When the owners learned that we were Indians, they said no. Would we be compelled to live in the slum?"

When Shattack asked her whether the bill would eliminate discrimination, she responded: "Do your laws against larceny, rape and murder prevent those crimes? No law will eliminate crimes, but at least you, as legislators, can assert to the world that you recognize the evil of the present situation and speak of your intent to help us overcome discrimination. There are three kinds of persons who practice discrimination: First, the politician who wants to maintain an inferior minority group so that he can

Territorial Govenor Ernest Gruening signs the historic anti-discrimination act in this 1945 photo. Witnessing are (from left) O. D. Cochran, Elizabeth Peratrovich, Edward Anderson, Norman Walker, and Roy Peratrovich.
Alaska State Library photo

station manager for Wien Consolidated Airlines. Throughout his life, he nurtured his growing family with subsistence resources, and one of his key goals in statewide leadership was to protect Alaska Natives' access to the land and its resources.

Degnan was a co-founder of the Alaska Native Industries Cooperative Association in 1947, and in 1950 he was elected as the first Yup'ik legislator in the Alaska Territorial Legislature. In the early 1960s, he represented Unalakleet at the first Inupiaq Paitot, a conference of northern Alaska indigenous people that focused its attention on aboriginal rights. Addressing the gathering, Degnan urged people to push for their rights: "You people here in Barrow, if you had your aboriginal claim, you would have gas today. And you would be collecting royalty from the people that come here. Standard Oil, the Army or Navy or whoever came. We were asleep when this happened. But today we are awake."

In 1966, he was one of the founding delegates to the statewide conference that became the Alaska Federation of Natives. Later, he testified in favor of Native land claims in Washington, D.C. In 1971, he was honored as the first AFN Citizen of the Year. The University of Alaska Fairbanks bestowed an honorary doctorate of public service on him on May 18, 1975.

Degnan died on Thanksgiving Day, November 27, 1980.

- July 4, 2004

May 17, 1906 – Native Allotment Act

On May 17, 1906, a law went into effect that has been described by one legal specialist as "the best kept secret the government has ever had." That was Alaska Legal Services Attorney Carol Yeatman's description of the Native Allotment Act, which was aimed at providing up to 160 acres of land to individual Alaska Natives. Its aim was to extend the Dawes Act of February 8, 1887, to Alaska. The Dawes Act actually led to a terrible erosion of the Native American land base as Indians lost their land over time. In Alaska, the Native Allotment Act led to Native control of land in the relatively few cases where Alaska Natives were aware it was a means through which they could gain title.

Although virtually all Alaska Natives were eligible to apply for land that had been used by their families and other relatives for subsistence purposes for generations, in the first 64 years of the act, only 245 allotments were approved, according to Alaska Legal Services. Most Natives were unaware of the law, and between language barriers and government red tape, those who did apply for an allotment often faced literally decades of waiting.

Passage of the Alaska Native Claims Settlement Act of 1971 closed the door on further allotment applications, although recent legislation authorized some Native veterans to select land after the 1971 deadline. The Alaska Federation of Natives honored Native veterans at the 1998 convention, and the allotment change was one of AFN's initiatives that year. The law authorizes the approximately 1,110 Native veterans who were on active duty between 1969 and 1971 to apply for allotments.

Nelson Angapak, Alaska Federation of Natives executive vice president, was one of the veterans who was granted an opportunity to apply for an

always promise them something; second the 'Mr. and Mrs. Jones' who aren't quite sure of their social position and who are nice to you on one occasion and can't see you on others, depending on whom they are with; and third, the great superman, who believes in the superiority of the white race. This super race attitude is wrong and forces our fine Native people to be associated with less than desirable circumstances."

Juneau's Village Street, where many of the state capital's Native people lived, is shown in this 1930s-era photo.
Central Council Tlingit and Haida Indian Tribes of Alaska photo

Juneau is only one example of the discrimination that took place against Native people. In Nome, Natives were expected to move aside if they encountered a white person coming toward them on the street. There, too, as in many other communities, Natives were relegated to a specific section of movie theaters.

Sam Kito, who was born in 1937 to parents of Japanese and Tlingit descent, says that when his Japanese-American father moved to Petersburg in 1934, cannery work was highly stratified, with Alaska Natives and Asians generally relegated to the less desirable jobs. And even if Asians or Alaska Natives performed the same job as non-Natives, they were paid substantially less, Kito said.

The 45 Aleuts of Attu Island, along with their two non-Native teachers, were captured by Japanese forces and most became prisoners of war. That was part of the official reason for relocating nearly 900 civilian Aleuts from the Pribilofs and other Aleutian Islands to crowded and unhealthy camps in Southeast Alaska. Additionally, Japanese Americans including among them some Alaska Natives were relocated during World War II to internment camps in the Lower 48. The effects on the Alaska Natives who were relocated were devastating, especially since many of them lost their belongings and eventually some even lost their homes. Many died.

Doyon leaders Al Ketzler, Sam Kito and Tim Wallace are shown in this 1960s-era photo.
Tundra Times photo

Although the effects of the war were less visible on other Natives, it had a tremendous impact on some villages. One village resident said the social fabric in the community began to unravel after the war. Many of the young men fought in the war, and when they returned, the village was less fulfilling for them. With less to do, some turned to alcohol.

Pressure on villages mounted greatly in the early 1960s with proposals for projects throughout the state that brought even greater numbers of non-Natives into Alaska. Among them were roads in Interior Alaska and a scheme to blast a harbor near Point Hope with nuclear devices. Writing in the book, *The Alaska Pipeline*, Mary Clay Berry discussed plans by the state to sell land claimed by Tanacross Natives near Lake George at the New York World's Fair of 1964. Claus-M. Naske's *A History of the 49th State* discussed the Rampart Dam, a stunning proposal to build a dam 530 feet high and 4,700 feet long at the Rampart Canyon on the Yukon River. The dam would have put "the entire Yukon Flats – a vast network of sloughs, marshes and potholes that is one of the greatest wildfowl breeding grounds in North America – under sever-

allotment as a result of the new legislation. He said he was pleased with success after lobbying for 26 years, but added that he felt a great deal of sadness for those who were not able to apply.

Angapak has applied for 160 acres near the village of Tuntutuliak in Southwest Alaska where he hunts.

- May 19, 2002

January 5, 1889 – Birth of Maj. Marvin R. "Muktuk" Marston

Marvin R. "Muktuk" Marston, whose creation of the Alaska Territorial Guard and reliance on Alaska Native leadership would have far-reaching impacts, was born on January 5, 1889, in Tyler, Washington.

A veteran of World War I, Marston had worked as a miner in northern Ontario, Canada. Because of his "bush" experience, when he returned to military service as World War II loomed, he was commissioned as a major and sent to Fort Richardson-Elmendorf in Alaska in early 1941. From the outset, Marston befriended Alaska Natives throughout the northern and western regions of the state. Unlike many others in the military, Marston had great faith in Eskimo leadership abilities and believed local people offered the best possible protection to the United States as a result of their strategic location, survival skills and knowledge of the terrain.

John Schaeffer of Kotzebue, who was born in 1939 and rose to the rank of major general in the Alaska National Guard and served in the late 1980s as commissioner of the Alaska Department of Military and Veterans Affairs, recalls that some of his earliest memories are of Marston's visits to his family home.

"My dad was one of his dog team drivers," Schaeffer said. "He said Muktuk was one of the toughest men he ever saw. Coming from a guy who lived out in the country his whole life, that was quite a statement."

Schaeffer said Marston was unusual for many reasons, not the least of which was his vision. His arrival in Alaska came at a critical time in history because the Inupiaq and Yup'ik people had just come through more than 50 years of change forced on them by the influx of non-Natives to

al hundred feet of water." Seven villages with a total population of 1,200 people would have been flooded, according to Naske.

Harold Moats and Col. Kenneth Sawyer discuss the Rampart Dam project as Fred John Sr. of Mentasta (standing) listens.

Al Ketzler Collection photo

In their continuing efforts to protect their lands, Interior Athabascans raised concerns about non-Native incursion in the region. Naske describes how Stevens Village Natives sought to gain their lands and were among those opposing the Rampart Dam. Tanacross Village Natives filed claims for their lands in the 1940s. In 1961, the Regional Solicitor of the Department of the Interior issued an opinion in which he asserted that "Indian title" was involved in a protest by the Natives of Minto, Northway, Tanacross and Lake Alegnagik. This was in reaction to state plans to establish a recreation area near the Athabascan village of Minto and to construct a road into the area to make it accessible to Fairbanks residents. The people of Minto eventually hired Ted Stevens, the man who would become U.S. senator for Alaska and eventually one of the most powerful senators in the nation. He offered his services free, according to Naske.

In 1961, many Inupiat joined together to form Inupiat Paitot to fight the proposed Project Chariot which called for using nuclear devices to blast a harbor near Point Hope. Howard Rock, who was originally from Point Hope, but who had moved out of Alaska, returned to the state and founded the *Tundra Times*, Alaska's first and only statewide Alaska

Native newspaper. The newspaper greatly aided the Eskimos in their fight against the nuclear project, and they eventually were successful in halting it.

By the 1960s, the effort to push Alaska Natives to the sidelines of their own state had become too much to tolerate. Native groups throughout the state united to fight for their land, and they were joined by a number of non-Natives who decried the marginalization of an entire group of people. In 1966, a major step in the fight for lands was taken when a statewide Native organization was created. That organization became the Alaska Federation of Natives.

Howard Rock is shown above at the 1975 Tundra Times banquet with author Lael Morgan and Gov. Jay Hammond.

Tundra Times photo

Many people credit Inupiaq Nick Gray, who was born in Nome in 1900, with being the spirit behind the first statewide gathering of Natives. Flore Lekanof, an Aleut who was elected as the chairman of the organization that became the Alaska Federation of Natives said Gray "really got us started."

"He was quite a philosopher in the Native way. He was a very deep thinking person and felt that without organization, the Native people would be swallowed up by the land grab of the new State of Alaska," Lekanof said. "Speak as one voice. That was Nick's philosophy. He said, 'If you don't do something about this, you'll lose it all. Get organized.' That was Nick Gray's push."

Just weeks before the statewide gathering of Alaska Natives that led to the formation of the Alaska Federation of Natives, Howard Rock wrote an

Alaska. Many of the changes to that point had been negative. But Schaeffer said Marston's development of the "Tundra Army" brought positive developments, including the organizational structure of the military and the introduction of armories which served to replace the traditional Native gathering houses which had been shut down by the missionaries.

"What he did was bring back control to the people," Schaeffer said. Before Marston's death in 1980, the National Guard Armory in Kotzebue was named after him. Besides his many military achievements, Marston worked for years to develop agriculture in remote areas, including a homestead he maintained at Unalakleet. He served as one of 55 delegates to Alaska Constitutional Convention from November 1955 to February 1956. He details his war years in his book, "Men of the Tundra, Eskimos at War."

- January 9, 2005

Inupiaq leader William Beltz was the first president of the Alaska State Senate.
Arne Beltz photo

April 17, 1912 – Birth of William Ernest Beltz

William Ernest Beltz, the first president of the Alaska State Senate, was born at Haycock on April 17, 1912. Beltz was the son of a Pennsylvania miner who moved to the Seward Peninsula in the Yukon Gold Rush of 1897 and an Inupiaq mother, Jack Skyles Beltz and Susie Goodwin Beltz. He was one of the couple's seven children who were raised in the mining communities of Haycock and Candle in Northwestern Alaska.

Beltz, a Unalakleet Democrat, died as a result of a malignant brain tumor on Nov. 21, 1960, while serving in the Alaska State Senate as the newly created state made the transition from territory to state. He was only 48 years old. He collapsed on the floor of the Senate in March 1960, but he returned to his Senate post within hours and completed the legislative session.

editorial in the July 29, 1966, issue of the *Tundra Times* discussing the importance of the land to the state's indigenous peoples:

". . .land to them is of deep regard which comes very close to being that of a religious reverence. This land is of deep significance, a heritage that has enabled them to survive for a great long period. The Native people feel very close to the lands they have continually used for ages. . .The land problem is of profound gravity to those people who have had the experience of living in the terrain intimately. They have received nourishment from it, buried their loved ones, raised their children upon it, developed their traditions and cultures, and established colorful stories and legends of the lands they have always known. It is when this tie to the country and terrain is threatened that the Native people of Alaska become alarmed because it is the only land in which they have indisputable ties."

Before the decade of the 1960s had ended, Alaska Natives had officially filed claims to 337 million acres of Alaska's 375 million acres, and the Alaska Federation of Natives had mounted a full-scale effort to gain title to Native lands. At the same time, state officials were filing claims to some of the Alaska Natives' most important lands because the state had been granted 104 million acres under the Alaska Statehood Act of 1958.

In the mid-1960's, Interior Secretary Stewart Udall refused to grant the State of Alaska title to land the state selected because of Native protests. This became a policy of a "land freeze" by 1966 that was a moratorium on the process of conveying state land in order to preserve the status of Alaskan lands until the Native claims were settled. When vast oil reserves were dis-

Roger Lang presents an oosik to Stewart Udall in this 1976 photo.
Tundra Times photo

covered at Prudhoe Bay in 1967, developers and state officials were unwavering in the fight to lift the freeze.

By 1966, three critical pieces had to be put together in the fight for passage of the Alaska Native Claims Settlement Act: a statewide organization, money, and a statement that clearly articulated the issue.

- The organization – the dream of Inupiaq Nick Gray, who worked tirelessly to organize Alaska Natives throughout the state – became the Alaska Federation of Natives.
- Money was provided in part by the Native Village of Tyonek when villagers shared some of their oil lease funds.
- And the statement was a paper written by Willie Hensley from Kotzebue who explained why Alaska Natives had rights to – and not just a need for – their lands.

Attorney Stanley McCutcheon represented the Tyonek Indians and helped secure $12 million for them for oil and gas leases sold to Standard Oil Company of California.
Anchorage Museum of History and Art photo

Without the generous financial assistance of the Native Village of Tyonek, the Alaska Federation of Natives would have been hard-pressed to gather Native people together from throughout the state. The village made a grant of $150,000 to AFN, as well as a loan of $100,000.

Hensley's paper tracked the historical and legal trail of Alaska Native land claims. In it, he detailed the legal situation facing Alaska Natives at that point and discussed laws that had been enacted after Alaska was purchased from Russia by the United States. The paper was responsible for helping to educate non-Native Alaskans and those in the Lower 48 about Alaska Natives' rights, as well as putting Native claims into perspective for many Alaska Natives.

A carpenter by trade, Beltz served as business agent for the carpenters union covering Northwest Alaska. He was first elected to the Alaska Territorial Legislature as a member of the House of Representatives in 1949 and began his service in the Senate two years later. He lived in Fairbanks before moving to Unalakleet in 1957.

As a legislator, Beltz was particularly concerned with labor issues, as well as social concerns of Alaska Natives. He was noted for his expertise in parliamentary procedure and worked well with legislators from both parties.

"They respected him," said his widow Arne Beltz, who is retired and today lives in Anchorage. "Some people even talked about him running for governor."

One of his daughters, Carolyn Beltz Terry of Nome, recalled her father as a kind man. When she was a child, he would take her with him on carpentry union jobs, she said. She recalled that he was an outgoing person, but a man who listened closely to people.

The Nome-Beltz High School in Nome, which has an enrollment of about 300 students in grades 7-12, is named after Beltz.

The family's early life is discussed in the book *Our Stories, Our Lives,* by Beltz's sister, Laura Beltz Wright, who established Laura Wright Alaskan Parkys.

- April 18, 2004

November 17, 1961 – Native Rights' Gathering in Barrow

"We the Inupiat have come together for the first time ever in all the years of our history," began a policy statement adopted Nov. 17, 1961, by the more than 200 Inupiat people who gathered in Barrow for a Native rights conference.

The gathering was named Inupiat Paitot, and it was supported in part by the Association on American Indian Affairs, based in New York. Accounts of the first Inupiat gathering are included in a number of sources, including *Alaska Native Land Claims* by Robert D. Arnold and *The Firecracker Boys* by Dan O'Neill. Arnold and O'Neill note that two of the key reasons for the formation of the Inupiat organization were mounting anger and frustration felt by Native people over proposed plans to detonate a nuclear device at Cape Thompson, near Point Hope, as well as limitations on hunting ducks.

In his account of the formation of the organization, O'Neill calls the opening words of the Inupiat policy statement "hauntingly reminiscent of the cries for aboriginal rights voiced by the American Indian a century earlier: We always thought our Inupiat Paitot was safe to be passed down to our future generations as our fathers passed down to us. Our Inupiat Paitot is our land around the whole Arctic world where we Inupiat live, our right to hunt our food any place and time of year as it has always been, our right to be great hunters and brave independent people, like our grandfathers, our right to the minerals that belong to us in the land we claim. Today our Inupiaq Paitot is called by white men aboriginal rights."

The Barrow gathering of Inupiat Paitot in 1961 was followed the next year by a similar gathering in Kotzebue. By that time one of the recommendations of the first gathering had been realized with

Emil Notti was president of the Alaska Federation of Natives during key early years of lobbying for the Alaska Native Claims Settlement Act.

Tundra Times photo

It was titled: "What Rights to Land Have the Alaskan Natives?"

At the time he wrote the paper, Hensley was 24 years old. By the time he was 26 years old in 1968, he had been elected to the Alaska House of Representatives, and he was serving as chairman of the Task Force on Native Land Claims, which had been created by Gov. Wally Hickel. Hensley found himself testifying in the historic hearings held in Anchorage February 8, 9 and 10, 1968, by the Senate Committee on Interior and Insular Affairs. As part of his testimony, Hensley's paper was printed in the hearing record.

In his paper, Hensley analyzed the flaws in assumptions made by Congress in the late 19th and early 20th centuries, specifically in efforts to turn Indians into farmers through the General Allotment Act of 1887, which was extended to Alaska in the Native Allotment Act of 1906.

". . .the Government still was dealing with the Native on an individual basis and was not allowing for the tribal nature of various groups, their common conceptions of land use and had made a significant retreat from earlier proposals designed to allow the Natives sufficient large areas for the continuance of their hunting, trapping and fishing economies," Hensley wrote.

Hensley referred to the fact that many Alaska Natives were only beginning to understand just how much of the state non-Natives were taking from them and what was at stake throughout Alaska. He noted that they realized they had to make rights assertions "over those lands which we have wrung a living out of for thousands of years."

Hensley's paper helped to galvanize Alaska Natives, putting into writing their concerns about an emotional and spiritual issue.

Proposals for settling Alaska Native claims were viewed by many – especially non-Native supporters of settling the claims – as a "bridge" that would help integrate Alaska Natives into the state's economy.

On Oct. 21, 1967, delegates of the newly created Alaska Federation of Natives adopted a constitution and bylaws. A year earlier, then-president of the Cook Inlet Native Association, Emil Notti, had called a statewide meeting of Alaska Natives in Anchorage. With assistance from Tyonek leaders, the meeting he called drew an estimated 250 people for a three-day conference with particular emphasis on Native land claims.

"The meeting in 1966 was momentous in that it was the first statewide gathering of Alaska Natives in history. By that I mean that we had representation there from every major tribal group and that had not occurred before. We were united in the face of massive land selections authorized under the Statehood Act. We saw that not only were our lands at risk, but so was our future as distinct peoples of Alaska," Hensley said.

The new organization's land claims committee was chaired by Hensley, who became the head of the organization in the early 1970s, after the passage of the Alaska Native Claims Settlement Act.

Hensley said Alaska Natives needed AFN as a united platform from which Alaska Natives could pursue their land claims. He said Native people understood "the unfortunate economic and social circumstances we found ourselves in at the time."

The constitution adopted in 1967 brought together Native peoples in a common cause of pursuing their rights not only as Natives but as citizens seeking justice for their land claims. Hensley said Alaska Natives also sought a better understanding of their unique cultures and values by other Alaskans.

The bylaws authorized membership in AFN by any member enrolled in a village or areawide association. Each village was allowed a delegate, and each areawide association was permitted a delegate for each 100 members.

the birth of the *Tundra Times* newspaper, founded and edited by Inupiaq Howard Rock of Point Hope. Eventually, these gatherings and others helped to raise consciousness on Native rights in Alaska and helped generate the historic land claims settlement 10 years later in 1971.

- November 17, 2002

August 19, 1965 – Tlingit, Haida land claims

On August 19, 1965, Congress amended the Jurisdictional Act of 1935 at the request of the Central Council Tlingit and Haida Indian Tribes of Alaska. The act passed in 1935, introduced by Alaska delegate to Congress Anthony (Tony) Dimond, recognized Tlingit and Haida Indians of Southeast Alaska as a federally recognized tribe to pursue claims to their ancestral lands in the U.S. Court of Claims. This was necessary because only tribes can pursue aboriginal land claims against the United States; individual citizens cannot. Although the Court of Claims could not grant land to the Alaska Natives, it could make monetary awards.

It wasn't until 1968 that the Court of Claims finally made an award to the Tlingit and Haida people, granting $7.5 million to lands withdrawn to create the Tongass National Forest and Glacier Bay National Monument.

The history of the Central Council of Tlingit and Haida Indian Tribes of Alaska has been documented by the council in a book titled *Central Council Historical Profile*, edited by Susan Stark Christianson, based on research and writing by Peter M. Metcalfe. The book notes that the history of the council is intertwined with the struggle of the Native peoples of Southeast Alaska for equal rights.

"The organization of the Central Council evolved out of the struggle of our people to retain a way of life strongly based on subsistence," it states. "That struggle included the rights of our people to claim lands we had used from time immemorial, lands we were given no claim to under the Western concept of land ownership."

Today, the council provides assistance to the Native people of Southeast through programs and services, including a Business and Economic Development Department, Education Services, Employment and Training programs, Housing and

"The first constitution was simple, but it allowed Alaska Natives for the first time to participate on a statewide level in their own organization. Its flexibility has allowed the AFN to continue its role as the pre-eminent representatives of the aspirations and interests of Alaska Natives," Hensley said.

Joseph H. Fitzgerald, former chairman of the Federal Field Committee, which developed a massive landmark publication that detailed the plight of Alaska Natives in 1968, favored settling land claims. And the publication Fitzgerald's committee developed, *Alaska Natives and the Land*, showed that from a Western viewpoint, Alaska Natives were fighting from ground zero. In 1968, Alaska Natives owned less than 500 acres in fee simple title and held only an additional 15,000 acres in restricted title. The study noted that some 900 Native families shared the use of 4 million acres of land in 23 reserves established for their use and administered by the Bureau of Indian Affairs. All other rural Native families at the time lived on the public domain.

Alaska Natives' urgent task in the face of the State of Alaska beginning its selection of land was to protect as much land as they could and make sure that it remained under Native control. Their aim was to give up as little as possible while maintaining as much traditional land as they could.

Although there was disagreement

Alaska's historic 1969 oil lease sale drew protests from Alaska Natives.

Tundra Times Photo

over what was to be accomplished by settling the claims, there was little debate about the situation Natives faced at the time. Throughout several years of hearings, witness after witness talked about terrible conditions in rural Alaska. In 1968, a number of witnesses compared conditions in many of the villages to Appalachia. But former Attorney General John Rader testified that even that comparison didn't go far enough.

"I noticed that they said in the Appalachia testimony – they said that the lack of adequate sewage treatment facilities turned some of the great assets of Appalachia into liabilities. The streams were polluted and so on and so forth. I was talking to a VISTA worker the other day and he said they did not have toilets, sewers, or even outhouses. The only trouble with the Appalachia comparison is that it is so mild," he testified before the Senate Committee on Interior and Insular Affairs.

At the same hearing, Frank Topsekok of Teller, representing the Seward Peninsula Native Association, pointed to the despair of the King Island villagers who had moved from their isolated island home to Nome:

"Today, the King Island villagers live in a terrible slum outside the Nome city limits. They no longer are able to live on King Island because the food is gone. They live in what Sargent Shriver called the worst slum in the Nation and have become a place where tourists are taken to see a Native village and poverty program experts come to make big plans and then go back to the cities and do nothing. Meanwhile, the rats from the Nome dump and the King Island villagers share the same housing."

An Athabascan raised in the Cook Inlet Region has described what it felt like to be an Alaska Native in the state in the late 1960's – before the Alaska Native Claims Settlement Act and after wave after wave of non-Natives moved to the state: "We were like foreigners in our own country." Flore Lekanof, AFN's first president, said discrimination was blatant in the 1960's: "The Native situation in Anchorage was not all that great. We were of the minority, and people looked down upon the Native people in those days. Oftentimes, the only time they were seen was coming in from the rural area, and then on Fourth Avenue, going from bar to bar. . .Native

Trust Services, a Human Services department and other special programs.

The offices of the Central Council are located in the Andrew Hope Building, which was completed in 1984 and houses the Alaska Native Brotherhood Hall, Camp No. 2 offices. Behind the offices is Village Street in downtown Juneau. At one time, many of the city's Native people lived in the Village Street area.

- August 25, 2002

Charles "Etok" Edwardsen Jr. was an outspoken advocate for Native land claims and eventually authored with Hugh Gregory Gallagher "Etok, A Story of Eskimo Power."

Tundra Times Photo

September 10, 1969, State lease sale

The state lease sale at the Sydney Laurence Auditorium in Anchorage on Sept. 10, 1969, netted Alaska $900 million and forever changed Alaska's destiny. In her book, *The Alaska Pipeline*, Mary Clay Berry notes that when the first sealed bid was opened, both BP and Gulf together had offered $15.5 million for one block of land in the Colville Delta. "There was a gasp of astonishment from an audience. . .The sale was off to a thrilling start."

Claus-M. Naske, writing in *Alaska: A History of the 49th State*, put the 1969 lease sale in perspective by pointing out that before that sale since statehood in 1959, Alaska had held 22 lease sales, all of which together netted less than $100 million.

Often pushed aside in looking back through the euphoria generated by the nearly $1 billion bid, however, are the mounting tensions leading up to the sale. A protest staged outside the auditorium by a small group of Inupiaq Eskimos was organized by outspoken Native advocate Charles "Etok" Edwardsen Jr. of Barrow. Although the Native leadership fighting at the time for passage of the Alaska Native Claims Settlement Act did not generally support Edwardsens protest, Southeast Tlingit leader John Borbridge said the Sept. 10 lease sale

people were stereotyped as people who were ignorant and drunk, walking the streets."

The Senate took the first major step in passing land claims legislation in July 1970, but the bill granted Alaska Natives only 10 million acres. Senator Fred Harris, D-Okla., led a drive to increase the land to 40 million acres, but his amendment failed on a 71-13 vote. In September, the House Subcommittee on Indian Affairs agreed to 40 million acres, but the committee failed to report a bill, so the question was held over, giving Alaska Natives "an opportunity to mount a strong campaign to build on their victory in the House Subcommittee," according to the January 1972 issue of Indian Affairs, the newsletter of the Association on American "Indian Affairs." The newsletter's summary noted:

"In April 1971, President Nixon met with AFN President (Don) Wright and publicly announced his own support for legislation that would convey to the Natives title to 40 million acres, thus assuring a Native victory in the Senate. (Only two months earlier Interior Secretary Rogers C.B. Morton,

Don Wright was president of the Alaska Federation of Natives Federation of Natives when the Alaska Native Claims Settlement Act passed.

Bill Hess/Tundra Times photo

testifying before the Senate Interior Committee, stated he would submit legislation conferring title to only 1 million acres of land.)

"The House and Senate Interior Committee labored through the spring and summer to produce one of the most complex pieces of legislation ever considered by them. In September both committees reported out bills for 40 million acres of land."

The Committee on Interior and Insular Affairs Report on the bill to settle the land claims, published October 21, 1971, noted that conditions faced by many Alaska Natives were appalling.

According to the report:
- The average age of death was less than 35 years; the infant mortality rate was more than twice the national average.
- Tuberculosis preyed on Natives at 20 times the rate for the rest of the United States. Other diseases ran rampant in Native communities, particularly those caused by environmental conditions.
- Alaska Native villages contained the worst housing in America. Of some 7,500 dwellings, 7,100 needed replacement.
- Out of 2,014 Native village households surveyed at the time, 1,561 had no water supply or waste disposal and 393 had well water only. Only 60 households had well water and sanitary waste disposal.
- Of Alaska Natives living in villages at the time, the average formal education was less than eight years. Those who wanted further education were forced to leave their communities and families – and in some cases even Alaska – for grades nine through 12.
- The 1960 census revealed that 21 percent of those in villages had no schooling, only 9 percent had completed high school and less than 1 percent had completed college.
- The Alaska Native unemployment rate was 60 percent.
- Annual per capita income for Alaska Natives was less than $1,000, much less than the official poverty level of the U.S. government.
- Legislation was developed under intense pressures – most notably the desire for oil development, but also the state's push to get its 104 million acres. Also, however, there was a growing

Alaska Federation of Natives President Emil Notte is shown above at left with Yakima Nation Tribal Chairman Robert Jim and two other members of the Yakima Indian Nation, which loaned money to the fledging AFN in its fight for land claims.
Tundra Times photo

demonstrated that Native demands for just compensation were not out of line.

Under the Alaska Statehood Act, the state was entitled to select 104 million acres of unoccupied, unreserved land from Alaska's 375 million acres. In the eyes of Alaska Natives, very little - if any - of the the land in Alaska qualified for selection, but despite their protests, by 1965, the Bureau of Land Management had transferred 12 million acres of the state, including Prudhoe Bay on the North Slope.

In late 1966, then-Interior Secretary Stewart Udall put a freeze on further transfers until Native claims could be sorted out, but the race for oil was on when Richfield Oil Co. discovered North American's largest oilfield at Prudhoe Bay in late 1967.

By the 1980s, oil taxes produced 85 percent of public state revenue, and Alaska's dependence on oil continues today.

- September 15, 2002

November 18, 1923 – Birth of Ted Stevens

Alaska's senior senator, Ted Stevens, was born in Indianapolis, Ind., on Nov. 18, 1923. A graduate of UCLA and Harvard Law School, Stevens was U.S. Attorney in Fairbanks. He has been an Alaskan since the early 1950s. He also practiced law in Anchorage and Fairbanks and served two terms as a representative in the Alaska State Legislature, holding positions of majority leader and speaker pro-tem.

During World War II, Stevens was a pilot with the 14th Air Force in China. In the Eisenhower Administration, Stevens was assistant to the Secretary of the Interior and Solicitor of the Interior Department.

Stevens will be remembered - truly even revered - by many Alaskans for many things. His leadership and selfless work on behalf of Alaska are unquestioned. And yet in his 33 years in the U.S. Senate, Stevens has established himself as a national leader able to hold his own in a global arena.

He has deep connections to the Alaska Native community, and he played a crucial role in the passage of the landmark Alaska Native Claims Settlement Act of 1971. Less known, however, is the fact that as a young attorney who had just moved back to Alaska from Washington, he took a case in 1963 championing the Native people of Minto. Working for free, Stevens helped the people fighting for their land and kept them from being mowed over by the Bureau of Land Management, the Bureau of Indian Affairs and the State of Alaska.

Writing in the book *The Alaska Pipeline*, Mary Clay Berry pointed out that at the time Stevens took on the case, the median income of the village Natives was then $1,204, and one in three Alaska Natives had no cash income at all. Stevens' early years in Alaska are also discussed in *Art and Eskimo Power*, Lael Morgan's biography of Inupiaq Eskimo Howard Rock, founder of the *Tundra Times*.

- November 18, 2001

realization within the United States that Indian treaties of the past had mostly been a license to steal lands from the nation's aboriginal peoples. It was time to do some thing new.

While Edna Ferber's novel *Ice Palace* did much to foster support for Statehood, Dee Brown's *Bury My Heart at Wounded Knee* is cited by many Native leaders as a key piece in gaining national support for Alaska Native land claims.

The proposals offered by Alaska Natives departed from past Indian policy. Rather than creating reservations, Alaska Natives were trying to craft a creative alternative to the reservation system in the Lower 48, which yoked people to the hulking bureaucracy of the Bureau of Indian Affairs. Rather than granting land and money to Indian governments, the legislation would set up business corporations to manage Native resources.

Edgar Paul Boyko, attorney general under Gov. Hickel, suggested setting up the task force in 1968 that led to the first version of the bill calling for the creation of corporations. Boyko had been married to a Jewish woman and fled Austria in 1938 to escape Hitler. When he moved to Alaska in 1953 to work for the Interior Department he was bitterly disappointed to find discrimination against Alaska Natives in Anchorage.

Boyko suggested the creation of the task force as a legitimate way for the state to finance Alaska Natives' travel to work on legislation and meet with state officials. "There was legislation pending, and the Native leadership really needed to have meetings all over the state, and this was a very heavy financial burden on some of them. And in order to make it easier on some of them, I proposed that we create a task force and appoint all the Native leaders and some of their attorneys to this task force because the state could then pay for their travel. And that's what we did."

The Task Force on Native Land Claims sought a 10-percent royalty on Outer Continental Shelf revenues and a royalty interest in some state lands. Alaska Natives later fought hard for some form of royalty continuing in perpetuity, arguing that since oil revenues came from lands claimed by Natives, they should share directly in the oil wealth.

The corporate provisions of the proposed bill emerged mainly as what was left over when traditional ideas such as reservations were rejected. They were the only feasible alternative to the creation of a reservation system in the state.

In her written testimony offered to the House Subcommittee on Indian Affairs in 1969, Inupiaq Laura Bergt strongly supported the creation of corporations.

"I believe it's extremely necessary for the regional corporation to control and manage our settlement funds. It's only reasonable that we should control and develop our resources from the settlement – and the most important one of all, the Alaskan Native. Who could be better qualified than we?

". . .I strongly urge you to weigh these factors and work towards vesting these powers to the regional corporation concept. This show of respect and confidence in the Alaskan Native will be truly appreciated besides showing wise judgment, understanding and faith in the Alaskan Native on your part. I'm confident that you will be extremely pleased with the capability, responsibility, and intelligence of the Alaskan Native in managing his own affairs."

For the Alaska Natives, lobbying was a long, slow process, and at the same time an emotional roller coaster.

The late Hank Eaton, who represented the Kodiak Area Native Association, recalled that after awhile it was "one damn door after another in this huge hall." Plane tickets to Washington, D.C., were sometimes paid for with the proceeds from bake sales, and leaders traveling to the East Coast often slept four to five people to a room.

In late 1971 the Natives' efforts paid off with what would become the Alaska Native Claims Settlement Act. For four long years, spirited debate had focused on just how much land Alaska Natives would be retained and how much cash they would be granted. The final bill that emerged promised 44 million acres and nearly $1 billion in cash.

After Congress passed the Alaska Native Claims Settlement Act, some

Native leaders gather in the office of Walter J. Hickel in the fall of 1970 while Hickel was serving as secretary of the U.S. Department of the Interior.

Alaska State Library Historical Collections photo

600 Alaska Natives gathered at the Alaska Methodist University for a special meeting called by Don Wright. Wright was originally from Nenana and served as President of the Alaska Federation of Natives during the final crucial year of lobbying. Gaining passage was a victory for the dozens of Alaska Natives who had spent countless hours in Washington, D.C., thousands of miles away from their homes. But when the gathering was informed of the news, the feeling at that time was more one of stunned resignation about what had been lost rather than excited elation about what had been retained.

Writing in a December 20, 1971, *Tundra Times* editorial, Howard Rock commented on the mixed feelings engendered by passage: "There was poignancy that would not quit that day. Great many of the Native people there probably experienced a sense of loss much more strongly than a sense of gaining. There were tears that threatened to spill that day. The atmosphere at the convention hall seemed to be prefaced with a special kind of sadness – a strange ending to a great fight for justice."

Speaking in interviews in 1999, Kodiak leader Eaton conceded that after the act passed a number of people were critical about the way it was developed. Many Alaska Natives said there should have been a broader base of support for ANCSA, with possibly even a statewide vote. "But that would have been impossible. . .The time element itself would have prohibited it. And the cost – who was going to dig in the pocket for the money to take a poll of all of the Native people in Alaska? It was just completely out of the question," Eaton said. "Those of us that were there – we did the best we could. I think we did a remarkable job when you stop to consider it."

With passage of the act, Congress took away most of Alaska Natives' land. Alaska Natives retained 44 million acres out of 375 million acres. The money granted was paid out over a period of years, which diminished its value due to inflation. Natives owned their land fee simple title, which was a shift from the government's previous policy of granting land in a trust status with the U.S. Department of the Interior. While it meant that Natives could sell what was essentially their birthright without seeking government

"There were tears that threatened to spill that day. The atmosphere at the convention hall seemed to be prefaced with a special kind of sadness – a strange ending to a great fight for justice."

— Howard Rock, 1971

permission, it also meant they would choose their own destiny in undertaking economic activities. Although the total amount of cash granted sounded like a lot of money, it meant that Alaska Natives failed in their attempt to get an overriding royalty in perpetuity.

It's important to point out that while many in the non-Native community viewed ANCSA as a "generous" grant, to Alaska Natives what was given up overshadowed what was gained. As Wright had testified earlier in 1971 when he was urging the Senate to support a 60-million-acre bill: "We are not asking for anything. We are offering the U.S. Government 84 percent of our property. We are offering them. . . more than 300 million acres to satisfy the needs of others in the state and to satisfy the needs of the United States in the way of federal reserves, wildlife refuges, wilderness areas. . .We will accommodate them all. We are asking merely to be able to retain 16 percent of our land in each region and we are asking for extinguishment of titles to the other 300 million acres, $500 million from the Congress and 2 percent royalty in perpetuity which will be utilized over the whole state of Alaska."

In the end, the amount of land retained was almost 12 percent, the cash was capped at $1 billion and special protections for subsistence purposes were left hanging. Significantly, ANCSA greatly shifted land ownership patterns in Alaska. Before the act was passed, only about one million acres (less than 1 percent of the total land and inland water mass) was in private hands. As a result of ANCSA, most private land in Alaska is owned by descendants of the aboriginal people, and most of that is corporately owned.

The fight for land claims required people to rise above their own personal needs and work with others despite differences in opinion and culture. Some of the Native leaders who worked closely together came from cultures that had traditionally been at odds – even war – with other Native cultures. And yet, they were united because the fight was an effort to end the victimization of thousands of people who wanted nothing more – and nothing less – than to hold on to their land and create a better world for their children.

"We are not asking for anything. We are offering the U.S. Government 84 percent of our property. We are offering them. . .more than 300 million acres to satisfy the needs of others in the state and to satisfy the needs of the United States in the way of federal reserves, wildlife refuges, wilderness areas. . .We will accommodate them all. We are asking merely to be able to retain 16 percent of our land in each region and we are asking for extinguishment of titles to the other 300 million acres, $500 million from the Congress and 2 percent royalty in perpetuity which will be utilized over the whole state of Alaska."

— Don Wright, 1971

A number of Native leaders have noted that the act was an experiment on a grand scale, and it was a radical departure for Congress, which in the past had dealt with indigenous people with treaties that were eventually broken. And, of course, a key difference between a treaty and an act of Congress is that treaties are not altered over time, but acts can be amended whenever the need arises.

Thirty years ago it was Native ties to the land and a desire to control their own destiny that spurred Native leaders to make innumerable sacrifices to get ANCSA passed. Far too many Native leaders to mention stepped forward to fight for the rights of Alaska Natives by sacrificing their time, their energy and their own financial resources. Non-Natives as well, joined together with Alaska Natives to speak out in favor of a fair settlement of Alaska Native claims.

Today there are several hundred Native corporations, non-profit organizations and other entities that are a direct result of ANCSA. ANCSA is not the basis for all Native organizations and entities, but a large number of them flowed out of ANCSA's passage. Its strength rests in how firmly it is anchored in Alaska. Alaska is the landscape where countless cultural beliefs and traditions are nurtured.

ANCSA was a far-reaching decision by Congress to deal with Alaska's Native peoples in a manner different than that used to settle Indian disputes in the Lower 48 states. It was the first piece of legislation aimed at real Native self-determination. At the time it was passed, the Bureau of Indian Affairs ran virtually all programs having anything to do with Indians and Alaska Natives. Back then, most people expected a government answer to a problem they rarely took the time to understand.

Former CIRI Chief Operating Officer Mark Kroloff has said that the Alaska Native Claims Settlement Act has become the biggest minority success story of the nation. And while many people have pointed to current social problems within the Alaska Native community, Kroloff notes that the act was never intended to solve all the problems. He believes that over time Native corporation leaders themselves have shaped the act through major amendments. He says they have a far-reaching goal: to develop enduring institutions that continue to meet the needs of the Native community and foster pride in Native cultures.

As Kroloff notes, the corporations created under ANCSA are looking to the long-term future in creating these institutions that may well live long after the corporations. In the case of CIRI, some of these institutions include the Alaska Native Heritage Center and The CIRI Foundation, which has an endowment of well over $50 million.

ANCSA was not a perfect system. On the other hand, Native Elders and the Native leaders at the time, most of whom were quite young, did the best they could with the tools they had to work with. Part of the beauty of their work is that the act they created is an evolving agreement. As a matter of fact, many, many issues have arisen since its passage, and many changes have been made to it.

What makes Native corporations so different from other business enterprises is that they concern themselves with the "real economic and social needs of Natives." These very words were at the heart of what ANCSA was in 1971 and remain so to this day. While there have been many strides in improving the lives of Alaska Natives in every part of the state, still many people continue to deal with serious problems.

Attorney David Case, who specializes in Alaska Native law, feels that the act overall has had a positive impact on Alaska and Alaska Native people. And he says Native people have made the act part of their own cultures. For example, he noted that Native people have a relationship to the land that goes beyond land as property and the basis for raising capital. In other words, many decisions made by corporations have focused on protecting land as the landscape for subsistence, as opposed to using it for its highest economic value.

CIRI President & CEO Margie Brown believes that the act is a tool, not an answer in itself. She said Native leaders may have been naive early on in the ANCSA process to think that corporations could address many of the major issues facing the Native community. And yet, she also said that the

July 9, 1982 – The CIRI Foundation established

Since The CIRI Foundation was established as a private foundation on July 9, 1982, by CIRI, nearly 2,300 individuals have received scholarships or grants totaling more than $7.4 million from the foundation. The CIRI Foundation granted its first scholarships in 1983 to 17 students, totaling $24,525. Today, the foundation has an endowment of about $47 million.

In addition to providing scholarships, The CIRI Foundation's mission is to enhance the heritage of Alaska Natives through programs that foster appreciation and understanding of Alaska Native cultures. For example, the foundation has provided heritage project grant funds to the Ya Ne Dah Ah School in Chickaloon, which received national recognition by Harvard University. In addition, the foundation supports books and videos. Since 1986, the foundation has published or assisted with publication of six books that provide readers with a better understanding of Alaska Native cultures by recording relevant events in history or through the sharing of stories and opinions of the elders and the young, aspiring leaders of tomorrow.

"For me, these publications are a great resource to learn more about my own heritage," says Automme Anderson, a CIRI descendant of Athabascan heritage. "They are filled with valuable stories and information that connects me to my own heritage and the rich Native culture."

The first book published by the foundation was *Our Stories, Our Lives*, a collection of personal experiences and traditional stores told by 23 Alaska Native Elders enrolled to CIRI who represent the major geographic areas of Alaska. The book was re-issued by the foundation in 2002 and is still sold in bookstores.

"The stories and words of these elders serve as a way of providing instruction and a meaningful way to pass on Native ways, especially our stories," says Susan A. Anderson, M. Ed., president and chief executive officer of The CIRI Foundation and a CIRI original enrollee of Tlingit heritage.

Proceeds from the sales of the publications go to the foundation to support its programs. Although the publications represent a relatively small part of the foundation's budget, they are a vital link in the foundation's efforts to record and preserve Native cultures.

- July 11, 2004

creation of Native corporations has led to tremendous economic and political strength for Alaska Native people.

First Alaskans Institute staff member George Irvin agrees, saying that the greatest benefits of the act have been the employment opportunities and political power that have flowed from it. It is a tool that has created jobs, as well as power.

Stephen Haycox, University of Alaska Anchorage history professor, said he believes that the corporate structure created under ANCSA encourages cooperation within the state and may even go so far as to prevent Alaska Natives from adopting a political agenda that walls off the Native community from the broader community. Haycox even suggested that the act has had the singular effect of saving Alaska from divisions that could have torn the state apart.

As it was passed, ANCSA had major structural flaws, and the Native leadership knew it. It was just vague enough that government officials almost got away with trying to unravel it in its early years of implementation. It contained a 20-year "time bomb" because it called for Natives to be allowed to sell the stock in their Native corporations after 1991. It required Native corporations to share resource revenues with each other, but failed to detail how that would be accomplished. It forced a Western system of individual rights on tribal peoples. Over the next three decades, the Native leadership had no choice but to deal with each of these issues.

Rasmuson sought prompt, generous Native settlement

Gaining passage of the Alaska Native Claims Settlement Act required united support from a wide range of people, both Native and non-Native. In 1968, the late Elmer Rasmuson, who at the time was serving as chairman of the board of the National Bank of Alaska, took an early leadership role in the Alaska business community when he stated his support for settlement of Alaska Native land claims.

"It was an unresolved situation, and the Natives were entitled to have it settled. We all needed to have it settled and for the reasons that I gave in my testimony, I felt that it was beneficial for the entire state. I don't think I can say it any better," Rasmuson said in an interview in his Anchorage office.

He offered his testimony at historic hearings held Feb. 8-10, 1968, in Anchorage by the U.S. Senate Committee on Interior and Insular Affairs, chaired by Sen. Henry M. Jackson. At the hearings, the Governor's Task Force on Native Land Claims, appointed by then Gov. Wally Hickel, unveiled their proposal for settling Native land claims. Hickel's Attorney General Edgar Paul Boyko had suggested the creation of the task force in order for the state and Alaska Natives to find common ground. The legislative committee of the Task Force, headed by Willie Hensley, included Emil Notti, John Borbridge Jr., Alice Brown, Richard Frank, Charles Franz, Byron Mallott, Hugh Nicholls, Harvey Samuelsen and Don Wright.

At the time he testified, Rasmuson had recently completed a three-year term as mayor of Anchorage and was serving as President of the University of Alaska Board of Regents.

"I am here and I believe I can make my best contribution in the testimony by emphasizing the value that will accrue to all Alaskans by a prompt and generous settlement of the Native land claims," he said in his testimony. "The benefit is from both a material and human standpoint."

He said the proposed bills to settle Native claims were not "special interest legislation," but rather that everyone would gain from the "preservation of the finest human values for all."

"This settlement should be treated not just as the extinguishment of a debt – however legal or moral be the obligation – but as a social program of most practical application. The proposal involves the dedication of a significant amount of our material resources to enable a vital part of our Alaskan population to participate in our development and contribute their

Three of the Chief Executive Officers of CIRI-affiliated non-profits participate in Native dancing an annual Native potlatch. From left, Gloria O'Neill, Cook Inlet Tribal Council; Susan A. Anderson, The CIRI Foundation; and Katherine Gottlieb, Southcentral Foundation.

CIRI photo

Frank Ferguson served in the Alaska Legislature from 1971 to 1986.

NANA Regional Corporation photo

July 14, 1939 – Birth of Frank Ferguson

Frank Roslyn Ferguson was born July 14, 1939, in Kotzebue. Hailed for his deal making skills, Ferguson wielded his significant power gently and with quiet diplomacy and grace.

"He was very bright," said former Gov. Bill Sheffield. "He really did know how to use the system for his people as well as the betterment of Alaska."

After graduating from Lathrop High School in Fairbanks, he served in the U.S. Army as a personnel specialist from 1963-65. Throughout his life, he practiced the subsistence lifestyle and loved camping and boating. He served on the Board of Directors of NANA Regional Corp., one of 13 Alaska Native regional corporations, as well as a stint as president of the Alaska Federation of Natives.

Ferguson served in the Alaska Legislature from 1971 to 1986, including four years in the House and nearly 12 years in the Senate before he was forced to retire as the result of a stroke. Ferguson focused much of his attention on programs to benefit rural Alaska, and he is credited with helping to end the era of Native students being required to leave home for high school. He also worked on expanding rural court systems, public

leadership. The greatest undeveloped resource we have in Alaska today is our Native population.

"What are these benefits? First, there would be the material wealth which would be utilized in Alaska. The Natives are permanent residents of Alaska. The settlement needs to be generous, because we all know that it is the surplus over our subsistence that is saved and re-invested. Thus the Native population becomes a strong contributory force to our economy which in turn would generate new business, broaden our tax base, and create additional investments.

"The second great benefit is the full participation of the people most concerned. This program furthers private initiative. The Natives have demonstrated their own great capacity and they need the tools to do the job.

"The third gain, and is to all our Alaskans, is the contribution of the Native leadership. This is possible only when the Natives have the confidence of their own wealth and the practice of their own management.

"I maintain that a new and substantive approach is necessary to achieve the desired results of prompt introduction into our Alaska economy and society of the dynamic cultural, spiritual, and economic force of a very great developing people. Delay is costly to us all in escalating price and lost productivity."

It would take four long years before the Alaska Native Claims Settlement Act would become law on December 18, 1971. But it is likely the early strong support of leaders such as Rasmuson went a long way toward ensuring passage of the historic legislation.

Ruby Tansy John, ANCSA advocate, dies

Ruby Tansy John testified at the first Native land claims hearings.
Jay John photo

An outspoken advocate for Alaska Native land claims died August 9, 1999, at the Alaska Native Medical Center. Funeral services were August 14 in Cantwell for Ruby Tansy John, 55, who died of a long illness.

Mrs. John was respected throughout the Ahtna Region, but she also deserves statewide honor for the courageous stands she took in the late 1960's as an advocate for Alaska Native land claims. Gov. Tony Knowles ordered state flags within the Ahtna Region lowered to half-staff in her memory.

Mrs. John was born September 27, 1943, in Cantwell. She was a graduate of Cantwell Elementary School, West High School in Anchorage and the University of Alaska Fairbanks, where she earned a bachelor's degree in mathematics in 1966. It was at UAF that she became involved in Alaska Native politics. She worked for the Fairbanks Native Association and later served on the Ahtna, Inc., Board of Directors. She was an active member and past president of Cantwell Native Council.

Before she was married to her husband Alec John, she testified at the first congressional hearings held on land claims Feb. 8-10, 1968, in Anchorage and questioned why there was even a need for Alaska Natives to make a plea for what already belonged to them.

"I don't see why I have to be up here saying, give us back our land, when in fact the land is ours," she said.

The effort by Alaska Natives to gain title to at least 40 million acres could not be considered asking for too much land, she said. And she stressed that she was concerned about the future of rural communities such as Cantwell.

health and safety programs and improving rural telecommunications.

Ferguson was as well known to political insiders as to the people back home in his region. In a tribute to him after his death, former Anchorage Daily News columnist Mike Doogan had this to say:

"Here's the way I remember Frank Ferguson: Barreling down a Capitol hallway in a shiny, light gray suit, tie askew, shirt tail trying to climb out of his pants, a bunch of folded papers sticking out of his shirt pocket, a can of Coke in his hand, a smile on his face and a twinkle in his eye.

". . .Ferguson was one of the smartest legislators I've ever seen. The ability to put together big, multi-layer deals takes many things. One of them is a kind of genius. . .Another is integrity. Ferguson, a Democrat, had it and everybody knew it, no matter what their party." He died in Kotzebue in 2003 of another stroke.

- July 18, 2004

August 2, 1947 – Birth of Rosemarie Maher, Doyon leader

Doyon Ltd.'s only woman president, Rosemarie Maher, was born Aug. 2, 1947, in a canvas tent at a Nabesna River fish camp near her home of Northway in Interior Alaska. Maher, who also served for 21 years as a member of the Doyon board including 15 years as Doyon's chairman, died unexpectedly July 6, 2001, at age 53 after a heart attack.

As a child, Maher was raised in her traditional Athabascan Indian culture. She left the region to attend high school in Sitka and later graduated from East High School in Anchorage. She returned home in 1969.

At the time of her death, Maher had been president and CEO of Doyon for just 18 months, but her involvement in Alaska Native organizations and public service began when she was in her 20s. Although busy as a wife and mother of four children, she moved back to Northway and became active in the community.

Maher served on a number of local and statewide boards, including a stint as co-chair of the Alaska Federation of Natives from 1997 to 2000. She was a member of the Alaska Board of Game during the 1980s and early 1990s.

"Rose committed her entire life to the success of the Alaska Native people," said Robin Renfroe, friend and former Doyon vice president. "She was born to lead, and she left us too early."

Although generally a quiet person, Maher used her leadership positions to speak up for rural Alaskans, especially those still struggling with social ills in small villages. She was proud of the financial success of Alaska Native corporations and the key role they have come to play in the Alaskan economy, but she worked hard at finding

"Cantwell Village was really an Indian village. But, with the coming of the white people, it has become more and more a white village. My people have become 'whites' without even realizing it. My people still hunt, fish and trap, but more and more of them are doing whitemen's work.

"The future of Cantwell and other Native villages is very dim.

"Cantwell is already almost absorbed in the white world. The people do not want to stop progress but want to be a part of progress and benefit from it. But we can't benefit from it if we don't have title to our land.

"My people have always thought they owned the land. They never heard of the word 'title.' It is a white man's tool which the Indian never had. We are fighting for the white man's tool. We never thought that we needed any such thing, but we find that we have nothing without it in our present society. The white man has taken our land for the highways. They have even moved our graveyard. All of this happened because we didn't have 'title.' Homesteaders and the State are taking our land that we own, but don't have title to.

". . .We don't want reservations. We just want title to our land so that we can put it to economic use. The benefits we derive from the land will benefit all society, Indian and white alike."

Mrs. John was a co-owner and operator of Tsesyu Service Station and Time to Eat Restaurant in Cantwell since 1972.

Rosemarie Maher was the first woman president of Doyon Ltd.
Curt Madison photo

Leaders of Native regional corporations are shown receiving the first payments of the Alaska Native Claims Settlement Act cash settlement in this historic July 1972 photograph taken in Washington, D.C. Shown from left are: Alaska Lt. Gov. Red Boucher; Mike Swetzof, Aleut League; Jack Wick, Koniag, Inc.; Martin Olson, Bering Straits; George Miller, CIRI; Joe Upicksoun, Arctic Slope; John Sackett, Doyon; Robert Marshall, Ahtna; Cecil Barnes, Chugach; Robert Newlin, NANA; Bob Willard, Sealaska; BIA Area Director Morris Thompson; Sen. Ted Stevens; and Don Wright, AFN.

U.S. Department of the Interior photo

ways to harness the success to foster programs to assist all Alaska Natives.

Maher worked closely with Doyon's revered leader Morris Thompson, and was named president of the corporation after Thompson retired in December 1999. Her death was the second major loss of leadership for the region in less than two years. Thompson, his wife and daughter were killed in Alaska Airlines Flight 261 crash on Jan. 31, 2000.

- August 3, 2003

2. An overview of ANCSA

The people affected by the act, its structure, how money was distributed and how land was conveyed. . .

I. People
- 80,000 Alaska Natives alive on Dec. 18, 1971
  (including about 20,000 living in the Lower 48 and other parts of the world)
- One-fourth degree or more Indian, Aleut or Eskimo ancestry
- Amendments authorized:
  - Issuance of stock for those born after
  - Descendants are not limited by blood quantum

II. Structure
- 13 Regional Corporations
  (12 in-state; one created later for Natives Outside; size ranged from Ahtna—about 1,000 shareholders— to Sealaska—about 16,000 shareholders)

Ahtna, Inc.
The Aleut Corporation
Arctic Slope Regional Corporation
Bering Straits Native Corporation
Bristol Bay Native Corporation
Calista Corporation
Chugach Alaska Corporation
CIRI
Doyon, Ltd.
Koniag, Inc.
NANA Regional Corporation, Inc.
Sealaska Corporation
Thirteenth Regional Corporation

◆ Natives enrolled each received 100 shares of corporation stock
◆ Enrollment determined by either:
  ▪ Where the person lived at the time
  ▪ Where he or she was from
◆ ASRC, Doyon and NANA created stock "life-estate" stock, valid only during the shareholder's life, for all or some of those born after 1971
◆ 220 village corporations (Size ranged from a minimumof 25 residents to about 2,000)
◆ Natives enrolled each received 100 shares of village corporation stock; those who chose not to enroll to a village or did not have prior residency in a village became "at-large" shareholders
  ▪ Amendments passed in 1976 authorized mergers, and among them are:

Mt. Susitna is shown in the background of this 1941 photo taken by Otto Thiele of Alexander Creek.
Otto Thiele photo

March 1941 – Photo symbolizes village's history, tenacity

It was a beautiful sunny day in March 1941 when then 19-year-old Otto Thiele stopped briefly to take a photo of his snowshoes in front of Mt. Susitna. Thiele lived with his family in the village of Alexander Creek, a 25-minute flight northwest of Anchorage.

Alexander Creek's 42 members were granted official village status by the Bureau of Indian Affairs under the Alaska Native Claims Settlement Act of 1971. However, in the mid-1970s, the Alaska Native Claims Appeals Board issued a decision that there were not enough Natives enrolled to meet the required 25-resident threshold.

Continuing efforts to gain official village status today are Stephanie Thompson, president of Alexander Creek, Inc., and other descendants of the Roberts and Thiele families.

According to the classic Cook Inlet place names

reference book, *Shem Pete's Alaska*, the village was known as "Tuqẹn Kaq'" and was referred to as a "very rich location." The descendants of the original Dena'ina inhabitants were decimated by illnesses that hit the region in waves after contact with non-Natives, culminating in the devastating worldwide flu epidemic coinciding with World War I. The few villagers remaining are believed to have moved to Tyonek after about 1918.

Thompson said her grandparents, Carl and Marie Anastasia (Clark) Thiele, of German, Yup'ik and Athabascan descent, and their six children then moved to Alexander Creek in 1938. At about the same time, she said, the Roberts family, who are of English and Aleut descent, also moved there.

Thiele's snowshoe photo is used on Alexander Creek, Inc., materials. The late Thiele, a retired tug boat captain, said he took the photo after he removed the snowshoes made by his father. When he looked back, he was struck by the straight line made by his tracks.

Thiele had high praise for his father's workmanship and ingenuity. "He was an absolute perfectionist. Everything he built was beautiful," Thiele said.

For Thompson, the photo's meaning is simple: "I think about the fact that the snowshoes are pointing the way home."

- March 9, 2003

- The Kuskokwim Corp.
- MTNT, Ltd.
- Gana-a'yoo, Ltd.
- K'oytl'ots'ina, Ltd.
- Alaska Peninsula Corp.
- Choggiung, Ltd.
- Afognak Native Corp.
- Akhiok-Kaguyak, Inc.
- All Ahtna Region villages except Chitina merged with Ahtna
- All NANA Region villages except Kotzebue merged with NANA
  ◆ Two villages, Venetie and Arctic Village, distributed assets to the village tribal government
  ◆ Some former reserves opted for more land instead of cash

III. Money
  ◆ $962 million in cash distributed over 11 years
    ◆ In the first five years
      - 10 percent distributed to individual shareholders
      - Regions retained 45 percent
      - Remaining 45 percent distributed to villages and "at-large" shareholders
    ◆ After the first five years
      - 50 percent retained by regional corporations
      - 50 percent to villages and at-large shareholders
  ◆ Section 7(i) requires regions to distribute 70 percent of resource revenues from ANCSA lands to all 12 in-state regions
  ◆ Section 7(j) requires regions to distribute half of the 7(i) money they receive to villages within their region and at-large shareholders

IV. Land

- 44 million acres
  - 22 million acres of surface estate to village corporations (with the subsurface going to the regions)
  - 16 million acres went to regional corporations (including both surface and subsurface estate)
  - 4 million acres to former reserves where the villages took land instead of land and money (Klukwan originally opted for this provision, but village leaders later changed their minds)
    - Gambell and Savoonga on St. Lawrence Island
    - Elim
    - Tetlin
    - Venetie and Arctic Village
  - 2 million acres for specific situations, such as cemeteries, historical sites and villages with fewer than 25 people
- Metlakatla on Annette Island, a reservation established in 1891, was not affected by ANCSA

March 3, 1891 – Alaska's only reservation

On March 3, 1891, Congress set aside the Annette Island Reserve to create the Metlakatla Reservation. The reservation encompasses the entire island and includes 86,000 acres. It is located in Southeast Alaska, 20 miles south of Ketchikan. It was created for the 823 Tsimshian Indians who had immigrated to Alaska from British Columbia with their leader the Rev. William Duncan.

They arrived on the island on Aug. 7, 1887, and have remained a tight-knit community ever since. Patricia Beal, Metlakatla's tourism director, said the population today numbers about 1,680 people, more than 90 percent of whom are descendants of the first settlers there. Although a few Alaska Natives from other parts of the state and Indians from the Lower 48 have joined the community, Beal estimated that they comprise only about 3 percent of the population.

Beal said Metlakatla encourages tourism, and she estimates that about 6,700 people visit the reservation during the summer. Tours generally last from two to six hours, but Beal said there are bed and breakfasts and a local hotel for overnight stays. Visitors generally tour the historic tribal Long House and view cultural presentations there. The facility is 100 feet long by 50 feet wide and is constructed with Le Sha'ax, large cedar timbers. Visitors also can view more than a dozen locally carved totem poles, the Annette Island Packing Co., and William Duncan's home, built in 1891.

The Metlakatla Indians did not participate in the Alaska Native Claims Settlement Act of 1971. They wanted to maintain all of their land on the island and their status as an Indian Reservation.

- March 3, 2002

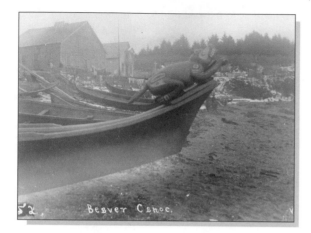

The U.S. Navy shelled, then burned the village of Angoon in Southeast Alaska on Oct. 28, 1882. Only one canoe survived the onslaught. Known as the Beaver canoe for the clan that owned it, it was the salvation of the villagers who would have starved that winter without it.

Alaska State Library photo

3. ANCSA Timeline

March 30, 1867 – Representatives of the United States and Russia sign the Treaty of Cession in which the United States purchases Russia's interest in Alaska at a cost of $7.2 million. The final sentence of Article III of the treaty deals with Alaska Natives, stating: "The uncivilized tribes will be subject to such laws and regulations as the United States may, from time to time, adopt in regard to aboriginal tribes of that country."

May 17, 1884 – President Chester Alan Arthur signs into law the Organic Act creating civil government in Alaska and providing funding for the education of the children of school age in the Territory of Alaska. The law provides protection for mining claims and lands used by missionaries, but is much less specific about Native land protection.

June 19, 1935 – Congress passes a special Jurisdiction Act, authorizing the Tlingit and Haida Indians to bring suit on their claims against the United States. The jurisdictional act was the first step in a long and difficult journey that led to the formation of the Central Council of Tlingit and Haida Indian Tribes of Alaska and ultimately was part of the basis for the settlement of all Alaska Native claims.

Jan. 3, 1959 – Alaska becomes a state and is admitted into the Union by presidential proclamation. When the state begins selecting the 104 million acres of land granted to it under the Alaska Statehood Act, Alaska Natives fear that the selections will have serious impacts on them despite disclaimers to the contrary in the act and the Alaska Constitution.

May 17, 1966 – Willie Hensley, Inupiaq of Kotzebue, writes a land claims paper, "What Rights to Land Have the Alaskan Natives" for a University of Alaska Constitutional Law class taught by Jay Rabinowitz. The paper is widely distributed among Alaska Natives.

Oct. 18, 1966 – First meeting to create the Alaska Federation of Natives draws over 300 people from around Alaska. The meeting is called the first Statewide Native Conference, and it is held in Anchorage through Oct. 22. The AFN will become the chief lobbying organization for the Alaska Native Claims Settlement Act.

Dec. 21, 1966 – The state director of the Bureau of Land Management in Alaska receives a letter from Secretary of the Interior Stewart Udall explaining his "land freeze" policy in Alaska. The secretary's action to suspend land disposal in Alaska because of protests by Native groups had been taken in November. The land freeze has the effect of halting state land selections, as well as development of the Alaska Pipeline.

Dec. 18, 1971 – President Nixon signs into law the Alaska Native Claims Settlement Act in which Alaska Natives retain 44 million acres (about 12 percent of Alaska's land area) and are granted $962 million.

Jan. 2, 1976 – President Gerald R. Ford signs the "Omnibus Amendments Act." The act makes amendments to ANCSA on issues ranging from supplemental enrollment of Alaska Natives to authorization of a complicated exchange of lands between the United States, Cook Inlet Region, Inc., and the State of Alaska. What makes the amendments especially important, however, is that they highlight the concept that ANCSA is a living document as opposed to a treaty.

Willie Hensley

Willie Hensley photo

Among those gathering for the 7(i) agreement signing on June 29, 1982, were standing, from left, Steve Hillard and John Shively; seated, George Kriste, Sam Kito, Agafon Krukoff Jr.
CIRI photo

Dec. 2, 1980 – The Alaska National Interest Lands Conservation Act, which is essentially an amendment to ANCSA, is signed into law by President Jimmy Carter. Section 17(d)(2) of ANCSA had called for the Interior Secretary to withdraw up to 80 million acres of public lands in Alaska for parks, forests and refuges.

June 29, 1982 – Presidents and CEOs of Alaska's 12 in-state Native regional corporations sign an agreement detailing how they will implement Section 7(i) of the Alaska Native Claims Settlement Act. The one-sentence section of the act requires that 70 percent of all revenues received by each regional corporation from ANCSA subsurface and timber resources be shared among the in-state regional and village corporations.

February 3, 1988 – ANCSA amendments are signed by President Ronald Reagan allowing for the continuation of Native ownership of Native corporations after Dec. 18, 1991. As originally passed, ANCSA called for restrictions on the sale of Native stock to be lifted 20 years after the act was passed. The amendments authorize stock sales only if a majority of shareholders vote to lift the restriction, and they provide automatic protections for Native land, as well as gifting of stock and issuance of stock to those born after Dec. 18, 1971.

Dec. 22, 1989 – The Alaska Supreme Court strikes down the state's 1986 subsistence statute as unconstitutional. The statute was aimed at a preference in the taking of fish and game for rural Alaskans in times of shortage. The ruling came in the case filed by Sam McDowell, who had been an ardent supporter of the 1982 Ballot Measure 7 to prohibit a subsistence preference in state law. At the time ANCSA was enacted, it was expected that subsistence needs would be addressed by the state. With the McDowell decision, it became apparent that would not be the case.

Dec. 29, 2000 – CIRI distributes approximately $314 million to its nearly 7,000 shareholder in an unprecedented special equity distribution. The distribution is $500 per share or $50,000 per 100 shares. This distribution is followed on May 4, 2001, with a second special distribution, totaling $94.3 million for CIRI shareholders in the amount of $150.29 per share or $15,029 per 100 shares. Together the two distributions are believed to be the largest total amount distributed by a Native corporation.

August 2002 – Akhiok-Kaguyak Inc. announces a decision to distribute most of a $40-million fund to its 147 shareholders, with shareholders owning 100 shares receiving two payments of $100,000 each.

August 13, 2004 – Groundbreaking for CITC Nat'uh/Non-Profit Service Center, the new home at 3600 San Jeronimo Drive in Anchorage, housing Cook Inlet Tribal Council, Inc.; Alaska Native Justice Center; The CIRI Foundation; and Koahnic Broadcast Corp.

Participating in ground-breaking ceremonies for the Cook Inlet Tribal Council's Nat'uh/Non-Profit Service Center were, from left, B. Agnes Brown, Ron Perry, Diane Buls, Chief Gary Harrison, John Crawford, Debra Morris, Susan A. Anderson, Diane Kaplan, Liz Connell, Charles Anderson Jr., Anchorage Mayor Mark Begich, Ed Rasmuson, Carl Marrs, Lu Young, Congressman Don Young, Gloria O'Neill, Joel Gilbertson, A. Debbie Fullenwider, Greg Razo, Roberta Oskolkoff, Clare Swan, Patrick Marrs, Christine Kashevarof, and Jaclyn Sallee.

CITC photo

December 9, 1973 – Roger Lang elected to lead AFN

On Dec. 9, 1973, Roger Lang, a Tsimshian from Southeast Alaska, was elected president of the Alaska Federation Natives, following Willie Hensley's term. Lang was born May 13, 1929, and died Dec. 30, 1987, at the age of 58.

Lang played a key role in the early implementation of the Alaska Native Claims Settlement Act of 1971 and served on the Sealaska Corporation Board of Directors beginning in 1972. In his honor, AFN named one of the annual President's Awards after him, the Roger Lang Youth Leadership Award.

Roger Lang
Sealaska Corp. photo

Nelson Angapak, who today serves as executive vice president of AFN, recalls Lang's tireless efforts nearly 30 years ago to promote cooperation within the Native community. Nelson said he was serving as chairman of Calista Corp. in the mid-1970's at a time when Calista had pulled out of AFN, along with The Aleut Corp. and Arctic Slope Regional Corp. Angapak said it was impressive to him that Lang always included representatives of all the corporations in discussions of key Native issues whether they were part of AFN or not.

"He always told us our strength is our unity," Angapak said.

Robert D. Arnold's book *Alaska Native Land Claims* included excerpts of a talk Lang gave in 1975 at a luncheon of Anchorage Republicans, predicting that someday an Alaska Native would

4. Early years:

Wholesale, unending, bitter struggle

Bureaucrats nearly derailed implementation of the Alaska Native Claims Settlement Act in the early 1970s when Alaska Native leaders were struggling to create and run their new corporations.

Former CIRI President Roy Huhndorf has described the first five years under ANCSA as a "wholesale, unending, bitter struggle."

Within months after the passage of ANCSA on Dec. 18, 1971, the Bureau of Land Management started writing land selection regulations designed to rewrite ANCSA and ignore congressional intent. Among other egregious provisions was a list of criteria for villages, which would have eliminated many villages from eligibility for land and money under the act. In addition, there were provisions which placed numerous specific easements and many "floating" easements on lands to be conveyed. This would have substantially decreased the value of Native lands and made management of trespassing almost impossible.

"We thought that they were supposed to be helping us, but the more we got involved with them, we found that they were adversaries. I'm talking about the BIA itself, the Department of the Interior as a whole. They threw just about every loop they could at our feet, I guess, and that's why it took so long to get some of these issues straight," Huhndorf said.

Native leaders met on a number of occasions with Rogers C.B. Morton, Secretary of the Department of the Interior from 1971 to 1975. Shown above in this early 1970s photo are, from left, Morris Thompson, Morton and Joe Upicksoun

Tundra Times photo

By 1976, the difficulties had mounted to the point that oversight hearings were called and the Native leadership united as a group to tell their story in Washington. In fact, the situation had the effect of re-energizing the Alaska Federation of Natives, which had begun to wither after passage of ANCSA. Many of the key leaders left AFN to work with the new corporations in their regions. By 1976, however, the leadership had come to the chilling realization that the problems created by the federal government threatened the very survival of the corporations.

"Since the Settlement Act was passed in 1971, the Natives have had to engage in an almost continuous struggle to prevent the Department of the Interior from using these provisions to chip away at the land rights granted them by Congress," Hensley testified June 14, 1976. At the time, he was serving on the NANA Board of Directors, and he spoke in oversight hearings before the Senate Committee on Interior and Insular Affairs in Washington, D.C.

Hensley's concerns echoed those raised by then-Alaska Federation of Natives President Sam Kito Jr., who testified on June 10, 1976, that the "countless delays, the arbitration and lack of definition affect the lives of our Native people every day and will surely affect their future."

The tasks before the corporations were tough enough without the leadership having to deal with federal conduct that bordered on malfeasance.

"The court record of litigations under the Settlement Act shows a consistent pattern of unlawful activity of the administrative agencies which has been set aside by the courts. That situation is not viewed by the Natives as a satisfactory way to administer the Settlement Act. Courts are both expensive and time-consuming. Administrative agencies should not require the consistent supervision of the judicial branch in order to obtain a lawful adminis-

John Sackett speaks at the AFN Convention as Willie Hensley looks on in this 1980 photo.
Tundra Times photo

head the Alaska State Chamber of Commerce. That prediction came true in 2001-2002 when Inupiaq Helvi Sandvik, president of NANA Development Corp., served a term as chairman of the state chamber.

Lang also predicted accurately that high-quality Native hotels would spring up and that Native corporations would become successful, "changing Natives' position in the state's economic and social circles." Lang seems prescient in that regard, too. The economic impact study of Native corporations done by the Association of ANCSA Regional Corporation Presidents/CEOs showed that in 2000, the 12 in-state Native regional corporations and 11 village corporations had revenues of $2.5 billion and assets of $3.4 billion.

But that wasn't the real measure of a better future, according to Lang's 1975 talk: "Most important is not these things, but the re-institution in the pride of being an Alaska Native."

- December 15, 2002

Tommy Pikok of Barrow and his grandson, Monyoyak, dance at the ICC gathering in Nome in 1995.

Bill Hess photo

June 13, 1977, First Inuit Circumpolar Conference at Barrow

On June 13, 1977, the first international gathering of indigenous peoples from throughout the world's northern regions opened at Barrow as the culmination of a dream to unite northern Natives by Inupiaq leader Eben Hopson, first mayor of the North Slope Borough.

Every four years, over a thousand Inuit from across the Arctic gather at the Inuit Circumpolar Conference's General Assembly to celebrate Inuit unity through dance, song and other artistic and cultural expressions. Since the first gathering in Barrow in the multi-purpose room of Ipalook Elementary School, others have been held in Greenland, Canada and Alaska.

The ICC was formed to represent the approximately 155,000 Inuit living in the Arctic regions of Alaska, Canada, Greenland and the Chukotka Peninsula in Russia. Since its inception, the organization has focused its attention on protecting

tration of Congressional acts. Natives should not be forced to expend their Settlement Act benefits in order to hire attorneys to obtain from the agencies the result that the law requires," he said.

John Borbridge Jr., then president of Sealaska Corp. who had been among those who fought for ANCSA, said: "no sooner does Congress giveth than the executive attempteth to taketh away."

Borbridge said that neither the spirit nor the intent of the law were being carried out: "Rather than looking first to the act to ascertain what Congress desired to accomplish by its adoption, the officers of the executive look first to other statutes and interests they are charged with administering."

Even under ideal conditions of cooperation with the government, Native leaders would have had their hands full.

Kito talked about the tremendous potential the Act had.

"The Settlement Act was hailed as an historic departure from the sad history of broken treaties with the Indian people. Congress indeed broke new ground; the Executive branch is sadly unable to respond in the same spirit.

"Federal agencies, primarily the Department of the Interior, continue to follow the path of the past. Promise the Natives whatever it takes in order to get their land, then break those promises to get even more of their land away from them," Kito said.

But still, he had hope for ANCSA's future. "History need not repeat itself. The time for fulfilling the promise of the Settlement Act has not passed. The Act can be saved and the treaty fulfilled if the Secretary will only decide to study the Act, understand its history, and administer it as a treaty of settlement with the Natives rather than some form of unjustified giveaway of Federal lands," Kito said.

Although important "omnibus" amendments to the act had been passed early in 1976, little had been done to speed up conveyance of land. According to the June 15, 1976, Alaska Native Management Report, less than one-half of 1 percent of the 44 million acres mandated to be conveyed had been actually conveyed.

Within the next two years after the oversight hearings, however, three more amendments were passed to ANCSA on October 4, 1976; on November 15, 1977; and on November 6, 1978. Although the amendments dealt with a variety of issues, ranging from CIRI lands to income tax provisions for Native corporations, the net effect of congressional action was to begin the process of convincing the bureaucracy that the implementation of ANCSA must be allowed to proceed. Gradually, the logjam on Native land conveyances was broken.

Federal bureaucrats nearly unraveled ANCSA in its first five years. Native leaders succeeded in preventing their rewriting of the law, but other major threats to ANCSA loomed ahead.

the rights and subsistence resources of northern indigenous peoples. The ICC's main goals are:

- To strengthen and celebrate unity among Inuit of the circumpolar region.
- To promote the human rights and interests of Inuit on an international level.
- To develop and encourage long-term policies that safeguard the Arctic environment.
- To seek full and active partnership in the political, economic and social development of circumpolar regions.

Eileen MacLean, an Inupiaq from Barrow, was elected as the first president of ICC. MacLean, who later was elected to the Alaska House of Representatives for Northern and Northwest Alaska, died in 1996. She said the first gathering was particularly inspirational because it showed how much northern people had in common with each other.

Her comments are documented in the book, *Taking Control*, by Bill Hess and published by the North Slope Borough in 1993. "We couldn't understand every word, but there was a bond between us," she said.

As ICC president, MacLean raised concerns about arctic health issues, such as water and sewer problems, and she noted that nuclear dumping was a critical problem that called for massive cleanup efforts. She also felt strongly that the ICC should focus attention on lifting travel and trade restrictions imposed on indigenous peoples.

- June 20, 2004

5. A Legacy of Sharing

Sharing was an ethic embedded in Alaska Native societies, and in every region of the state elders pass on stories of the importance of communal help.

Stella Martin, the late Tlingit Elder from Kake, recalls the sharing that took place in her Southeast Alaska village. Her father was generous, as well as sensitive to the shame those in need felt when they asked for help.

"Everybody helped each other. One of the joys of being a Tlingit is you're never alone. There's always somebody. You're never an orphan. When my father died, even though we were adults, people came forward and said, 'Remember, we are still here.' My father's clan of people: 'We are still here.' And when my mother passed away, the same thing happened. And we always had somebody we could go to.

For a funeral, everybody goes. . .Everybody just turned out. They built the caskets, and they were beautifully done. Finished and everything. Had a lining. And it was always a work of art. They didn't send out for any of that. There was no undertaker, of course. They had a nurse, and she generally alternated every other month. So even with sickness you had to learn to look out for each other.

Everybody helped each other. You were never alone. If somebody was running short of food – I remember people would come to the house and say, 'My children have nothing to eat.' And Dad would tell them, 'Come back tonight, and bring a sled.' He would tell them to come at night so that nobody would see. . .We always had a lot of food because Mother and Dad put up a lot of food. We always had enough to share with others. It was not considered welfare; it was just a case of helping each other."

The sharing concept made its way into the Alaska Native Claims Settlement Act through a one-sentence provision of the act, Section 7(i), that has been described as elegant in concept, but a nightmare in implementation. Although sharing was always a part of Native cultures, it was generally expected only within particular villages and more rarely between cultures. It is significant, therefore, that the sharing provisions of ANCSA require sharing among all Native corporations, crossing traditional ethnic boundaries.

At the same time, the sharing requirement is one of the most important distinctions between Native corporations and other Western business entities. Through Section 7(i), Native regional corporations share a large portion of their resource revenues with each other. Section 7(i) of the act states simply that 70 percent of all resource revenues received by each region from ANCSA lands will be shared among the 12 regional corporations within Alaska.(A corporation created later to represent Alaska Natives living outside the state, the Thirteenth Region, was not included because it was not granted land.)

A further provision of ANCSA calls for distribution of the shared funds to villages within each region and "at-large" shareholders who are shareholders of a regional corporation only and not a village corporation. Section 7(j) requires that regions then share half of the 7(i) funds they receive with village corporations and individual at-large shareholders.

January 23, 1967: Maniilaq serves Northwest Alaskans

Northwest Alaska's key social service agency, Maniilaq Association, was incorporated on January 23, 1967. The organization was initially funded by the statewide advocacy organization Rural Alaska Community Action Program, known as RurALCAP. Dennis Tiepelman, Maniilaq president and CEO, said Maniilaq's original funding of $50,000 a year came as a result of President Lyndon Johnson's "war on poverty."

Maniilaq is an outgrowth of the Northwest Alaska Native Association, formed by Willie Hensley and other Inupiaq leaders from the region. The association eventually was the basis for the creation of NANA Regional Corp., a for-profit corporation; Maniilaq; and the Kotzebue Area Health Corp. The name Maniilaq, originally spelled Mauneluk, comes from an early spiritual leader of the region.

Through the years, Maniilaq has undertaken a number of programs to serve the people of the region, most of whom are Inupiaq Eskimos. Because most of the people have relied on subsistence with limited access to the cash economy of the state, social service programs were vital and remain so to this day.

"One of Maniilaq's early contracts in 1969 was to administer the beginning payroll of the village health aide program from the Indian Health Service," Tiepelman said. "These health aides are now the respectable statewide cadre of community health practitioners, with two or more employed in each community." Today, Maniilaq has grown to the point where its annual budget is $50 million. Its mission remains the same as it always has been to deliver contract services by federal and state contracts in health care, education, social services and manpower training to the people of the region.

- January 27, 2002

The sharing requirements of the Alaska Native Claims Settlement Act are among the most "Native" aspects of the act. Through these provisions, more than nearly $675 million – an amount equal to more than half of the entire cash settlement of ANCSA – has been distributed over three decades to regional corporations, village corporations and individual shareholders.

Although the sharing requirement was generally supported by most of the Native leadership, there was never unanimous support for it. And there are still issues surrounding resource-revenue sharing among Native regional corporations. Even from the very beginning, it was controversial and always brought out naysayers.

Early in ANCSA's history, however, one of the Native regional corporations, NANA Regional Corp., made a decision to publicly distribute nearly $2 million. This gesture may have gone a long way toward making the sharing a reality. The distribution was both symbolic because it was done at a statewide Native gathering and significant because of the amount of money involved.

While the provisions may feel oppressive at times to the resource-rich regions, they have been important sources of income at different times to some corporations, even to the point of keeping some from bankruptcy. "Section 7(j) has proven to be critical in ensuring the continued viability of many village corporations as functioning economic entities because in many areas of Alaska, village corporations are heavily dependent upon section 7(j) income," Attorney James D. Linxwiler wrote in his legal analysis of ANCSA's first 20 years.

In the early 1970's, however, it was not at all clear whether the provisions would prove workable. In fact, 7(i) nearly became the undoing of the law. Although the language seems simple, it led to seven years of expensive litigation among the 12 Native regional corporations.

Some of the earliest versions of legislation that eventually became ANCSA called for resource revenue sharing. The 1968 version of the act developed by the U.S. Department of the Interior called for the creation of one statewide economic corporation, which in the case of mineral development would retain half of the revenues and distribute the other half to the village where the resources were located. Interior Secretary Stewart L. Udall testified that the provision was included because the department had considered the fact that there would be valuable minerals under some of the lands given to certain villages and not to others.

A similar concept for the sharing of resource revenues throughout the Native community was formally stated in late 1968 with publication of *Alaska Natives and the Land*, issued by the Federal Field Committee for Development Planning in Alaska. Among alternatives suggested for consideration in granting land to Alaska Natives: "Assigning revenues from mineral estate, if such estates in land are granted, on a pro rata basis to all the Natives of Alaska; this alternative would avoid the creation of 'have' and 'have not' villages."

Hank Eaton, a Native leader from Kodiak who lobbied for the law and who died in 2001, discussed the philosophy behind the provision. He said the Native leadership understood the fact that there would naturally be divisions between the "haves" and "have-nots."

"That was more or less the way we were looking at it when we were pushing this thing – we were looking at the time when we could all be pretty much on a par," he said.

Byron Mallott, former Sealaska Board chairman, believes the philosophy behind the sharing provision is sound, but that the addition of vague sharing requirements to the law came about as a result of the early leadership's inexperience in the business world.

"Seven(i) was a simple and elegant concept in establishing natural resource sharing equity among all corporations, but its implementation was an absolute nightmare. It was unique to ANCSA. . .It would never have been foisted on anyone else," Mallott said. Mallott's theory is that leaders lobbying for land claims legislation hoped to develop a settlement that would be fair and equitable to all Native people, rather than creating a system of competition with people fighting over "shares of the pie." And he

Mike Irwin, Chris McNeil, Ralph Eluska, Julie Kitka, Willie Hensley, Oliver Leavitt and Janie Leask are shown at a meeting of AFN officials in the mid-1980s.

Tundra Times photo

But he stressed that 7(i) can't be viewed through Western eyes in order for it to make sense. In the Native view, the focus is on what is best for the group, not the needs of the individual shareholder or even the individual corporation.

said it was easy to put in ANCSA because none of those involved in crafting the act were business people.

"There was an academic, theoretical – starry-eyed – view of what business corporations were and what they could do," he said. But to put the provision in perspective, Mallott asked what would happen to the airline industry if airlines had to share 70 percent of their revenues because the government believed there should be equity among them?

"Pose that question and it just boggles the mind. Even if you accepted the notion, how would you do it?" Despite the difficulties, however, Mallott believes the provision had the effect – eventually – of uniting Alaska Native Corporations.

Some scholars have suggested that the act itself "was designed to achieve an equitable distribution of land resources among Alaska Natives."

When revenue sharing was put into the legislation, the initial versions differed markedly in their approach to the sharing provisions that eventually became 7(i). Early drafts of the act required that the timber and subsurface resources be distributed on a population basis to all of the Alaska Natives in order that all Natives would share equally in the resource wealth of Alaska administered by a single statewide corporation. By contrast, a later Senate bill provided that only 50 percent of the revenues from the timber and subsurface resources would be subject to sharing. In the end, the Conference Committee adopted a compromise with the requirement to share 70 percent.

John Shively, former NANA Regional Corp. executive who was intimately involved in negotiations surrounding the interpretation of the sharing requirement, calls 7(i) the most nontraditional part of ANCSA.

"If you look at it from a standpoint of 'gifting,' or waste of corporation assets, it's one of the biggest gifting provisions that I have ever seen because those corporations that have assets. . .are giving away literally tens of millions of dollars for nothing," he said. But he stressed that 7(i) can't be viewed through Western eyes in order for it to make sense. In the Native view, the focus is on what is best for the group, not the needs of the individual shareholder or even the individual corporation.

Even so, the sharing provision began creating tension between Alaska Native regional corporations almost as soon as the act was passed. Corporations acquiring lands with natural resource potential hoped to interpret the sharing provision narrowly, while others sought for a different approach. Although the provision is a simple requirement stated in one sentence, it has been suggested that the complexities of implementation could be compared to a tax law which requires a certain percentage of income to be paid to the government, without defining the term "income."

In the first years of implementing the act, some recognized that the sharing provision of ANCSA was critical to the success of the act. "It is generally agreed by regional corporate managers that one of the crucial tests of the Settlement Act and ultimately the survival of the 12 regional corporations will be the workability of Section 7(i), according to the Alaska Native Management Report, which tracked ANCSA issues in the early years of implementation.

One of many problems with seeking answers in the courts is that since 7(i) is highly unusual, there is virtually no precedent to follow. A six-month study of Alaska Native corporations by Touche Ross & Co. in 1973, initiated by the Alaska Native Foundation, described the sharing provisions as "highly ambiguous and controversial." The report stated it was imperative that the corporations decide jointly on how to implement the sharing provisions of ANCSA because the only other two options for settling the issues surrounding 7(i) were through court action or government regulation.

Among others who predicted early on that 7(i) would fail were John Hanrahan and Peter Gruenstein, authors of *Lost Frontier, The Marketing of Alaska*, published in 1977. They quoted then-Doyon Ltd. President Tim Wallis saying 7(i) "impedes growth" through disincentives to corporate development of the subsurface estate. "Let each of the corporations fend for itself, "he said". After all, does Macys share profits with Gimbel's?"

The critics were prescient. Later, the publication *44: Alaska Natives Claims Settlement Act 1971-1979*, produced by the Federal-State Land

John Schaeffer, president of NANA Regional Corp., discusses NANA's decision to distribute revenue-sharing checks during the October 27, 1976, Tundra Times Banquet.

Jimmy Bedford/Tundra Times photo

". .it is our hope that, by making this distribution at this time, other regional corporations holding 7(i) revenues will do likewise, and settlement of the two 7(i) lawsuits will be encouraged and eventually may become a reality."

— NANA Letter, 1976

Use Planning Commission took note of the "considerable" litigation and suggested that the provision was failing:

"The various Native groups living in Alaska rarely shared things between ethnic groups before the arrival of the White man, and it is not likely that they will be eager to share statewide now. The proportion of proceeds to be shared may be especially difficult to give."

Some Native leaders, however, had high hopes for the success of 7(i) sharing and believed that the corporations could eventually resolve their differences. NANA Regional Corp. took the lead in this regard after the corporation negotiated an agreement with Standard Oil Company of California to drill three exploratory wells in the Kotzebue area. In an effort to encourage other Native corporations to end their lawsuits and share with each other, NANA Regional Corp. passed out checks totaling almost $2 million to the 11 other Native regional corporations within Alaska at the Tundra Times banquet on October 27, 1976. For the time, it was a large amount of money. The gesture was meant to be public and set an example, and its significance in cultures that prize leadership cannot be overstated.

"This check represents your Corporation's share, subject to possible adjustments, of the money which NANA has received to date from Standard Oil Company of California (SOCAL) and which is distributable under Section 7(i) of the Settlement Act, as well as your share of the interest due on your share of the funds. The total amount being distributed to the 11 Regional Corporations is $1,831,069.00. The method by which this total amount was calculated and your Corporation's percentage share are shown on attached schedules and explained below.

"We are making the distribution because the money involved clearly is subject to distribution under Section 7(i), and interest thereon. Although NANA has had possession of this money since it was received from SOCAL, it is not really ours, and we therefore have not considered ourselves authorized to spend it. . .it is our hope that, by making this distribution at this time, other regional corporations holding 7(i) revenues will do likewise, and settlement of the two 7(i) lawsuits will be encouraged and eventually may become a reality," stated a cover letter from NANA with the checks.

The letter went on to urge Native people to work together and avoid lawsuits: "Certainly we are charged with corporate responsibility, but there is a marked difference between good business practice and sharp and disruptive business practices. Good business practices need not destroy the Native spirit of unity."

A report prepared for Congress in 1976 took note of the serious problems created by 7(i), but included a comment by a Native regional corporation leader suggesting that the provision had the potential to eventually unite Alaska Natives by forcing them to work together.

Jerome Trigg, then president of Bering Straits Native Corp., said he supported the sharing provisions "since such a mechanism would create a network of communications and interrelationships among the regional corporations," according to the American Indian Policy Review Commission's "Special Joint Task Force Report on Alaskan Natives Issues." Trigg was prophetic in his suggestion that the provision would bring the corporations together, but it was years before that became a reality.

In practice, the disputes had serious implications for the newly created companies which generally had resources, but very little else. In a decision issued in 1976, District Court Judge James A. Von der Heydt decried the fact that the courts were so involved. "Unfortunately, the Congressional mandate, that the settlement be accomplished rapidly and without litigation. . .has not been fulfilled. There are numerous cases before this Court involving the interpretation to be given various sections of ANCSA. The Court can take judicial notice of the fact that the attorneys' and accountants' fees chargeable to the various Native corporations are a severe burden on their cash flow. It is primarily for this reason that the Court has undertaken this attempt to resolve as many questions as is possible, in a judicial context, concerning the meaning and application of Section 7(i)," Von der Heydt said.

In litigation filed in the first years of ANCSA, the two areas of contention were the kinds of revenue subject to sharing and deductions that would be

"Let each of the corporations fend for itself. After all, does Macy's share profits with Gimbels?"

- Tim Wallace, 1977

67

The CIRI Building is shown under construction shortly before its fall 1977 completion.

CIRI photo

allowed. By 1981, all 12 Native regions had become party to a pending case filed on April 4, 1975, by The Aleut Corp. and four other regional corporations – Ahtna, Inc.; Chugach Natives, Inc.; Koniag, Inc.; and Sealaska Corp. – against Arctic Slope Regional Corp. They claimed that some of the funds Arctic Slope received under exploration and development contracts with four oil companies fell under the provisions of 7(i). It wasn't long before numerous cross-claims and counter-claims were filed.

Also still pending at the time was a 1974 case filed by Doyon, Ltd., against NANA Regional Corp.

Special Master Ralph Wienshienk of New York was assigned to the proceedings in 1981 by Von der Heydt to develop a report on the proceedings. He discussed the history of the issue in his report, and noted that the courts were becoming increasingly involved the controversy swirling around 7(i) issues. "Both the United States District Court for the District of Alaska and the United States Court of Appeals for the Ninth Circuit considered and ruled upon a number of preliminary questions in this action clarifying certain fundamental ambiguities found in the revenue sharing provision," he said.

"Anyone familiar with the volumes of statutes, regulations and case law in the area of defining taxable 'income' would readily appreciate the challenge involved in agreeing on how equitably to implement a statutory division of 'revenues,' " Wienshienk wrote.

Sensing that the one-sentence sharing provision of ANCSA, which was a Native concept applied to Western-style corporations, could become the undoing of the act, Byron Mallott became concerned. At the time, Mallott was serving as the president of Sealaska, the largest Native regional corporation in terms of population and one with vast timber resources on its lands.

"We saw opportunities to make money from harvesting and selling timber to the Asian markets, but really couldn't proceed without some definition of what 7(i) meant. Several other corporations were in the same circumstance, and I can recall getting together with Roy Huhndorf. We were in all kinds of strife over it among the corporations. The litigation wasn't so friendly any more," Mallott said.

"CIRI and Sealaska had a strong self-interest in resolving it as we were first out of the box with resource development," Mallott said. But he added that there were other corporations with as much concern, but less urgency. Most notable were Doyon and NANA.

"So I talked with Roy and said, 'What if one of us invited all the other corporations to a place away from our offices? Let's see if we can stop the litigation and come to an agreement over how to deal with this 7(i) issue.' "

Mallott noted that at the time CIRI did not have the resources to host such a meeting, but Sealaska did, so corporation leaders were invited to the Kah-Nee-Ta Lodge on the Warm Springs Indian Reservation in Oregon in a March 10, 1981, letter sent out by Mallott. In his letter, Mallott noted that despite very high stakes, settlement efforts up to that time had not ended the litigation, which was a tremendous expense for all and with minimal results.

In extending an invitation to the Native corporations to attend the sessions, Mallott asked that the corporate leaders not bring their legal counsel to the meetings. Although most of the corporations did bring attorneys, counsel was asked not to sit at the negotiating table with the corporate leadership. Richard Baenan, an outside attorney who had worked for NANA Regional Corp., served as the legal counsel for the group.

Warm Springs was selected almost by serendipity. The goal was to have a two-day gathering on neutral territory outside of Alaska. One of the leaders had heard about Kah-Nee-Ta, and it was a logical choice to meet in Indian Country. The gathering included several representatives from each of the 12 Native regions within Alaska. Although the majority of those who attended were men, some regions sent female board members and staff members.

In 1981, the Native regional corporations were still getting on their feet, and people generally did not have extensive business educations or even business experience. Still, the leadership had had nearly 10 years of expe-

Native leaders discuss revenue-sharing strategies during their meeting in Warm Springs, OR.
CIRI photo

Willie Hensley, left, and Sam Kito take a break to relax during the revenue-sharing meetings at Warm Springs, OR.

CIRI photo

rience in getting their businesses started.

"There was a lot of discussion of the issues," said Shively. "It wasn't a meeting that produced anything other than agreement that this process should go forward. Different sides were able to express their opinions about the different issues. People were not yelling at each other. These were people who were generally friends and had known each other for years, through high school at Mt. Edgecumbe in Sitka or work on the Claims Act in Washington, D.C. Many of them had been trying to make it work ever since, and they sat on the AFN board together, which back then was a relatively small board," he said.

As a result of the Warm Springs gathering, consensus was developed to continue the process.

"And then we spent an entire year immediately following in a long series of negotiating sessions, hosted largely by CIRI in the CIRI Boardroom, which ultimately resulted in the 7(i) settlement agreement," Mallott said.

Throughout the year of negotiations, a mountain of paper was traded back and forth between the leaders. There were regular monthly meetings, as well as numerous extra meetings of various subgroups. But besides the tangible evidence that people were trying to work together was the intangible feeling of trust that would become the most important commodity in the process.

"Tons of pieces of paper kicked back and forth," Shively said. "I can't recall it all, but there were discussions about expense claims, agreements, definitions of revenues. As we started through it, there was lots of language. There were many drafts. As we went along and started to work through issues, the lawyers would draft the language, and we'd go over it. You'd just keep going."

Shively said there were many "sides," but generally speaking throughout the negotiations the key "haves" – Sealaska, CIRI and ASRC – often took one side and the more notable "have-nots" – Bristol Bay, Calista, Koniag and the Aleuts – another. He said in hindsight he believes that NANA's role as a "have" in favor of sharing was likely critical to the negotiations.

"NANA had resources. We were working on the Red Dog agreement at same time we were working on 7(i). We were trying to find a middle ground. We believed in the agreement, and I wanted the systems as much as possible not to be complex. For example in coming to an agreement on an overhead formula, we put thresholds in the agreement so that we weren't nitpicking people to death. You had to be arguing over serious issues, and if you were found guilty of misstating your 7(i) net revenues, you had to have a big penalty. If you lost, you had to pay at prime plus 5 percent."

The agreement requires arbitration, not lawsuits, in the case of disagreements that cannot be negotiated among the regions. Many observers believe this is one of the most significant aspects of the agreement. Shively said that over time, this requirement has saved significant costs, possibly tens of millions of dollars in litigation and accounting fees. "The whole agreement was about getting us out of court; if we hadn't gotten out of court, we'd still be there," he said.

What began as a tiny mustard seed at the gathering in Warm Springs and gradually grew throughout the year of meetings was trust. Could they trust each other? He said Mallott's key accomplishment in the process was in finding a way to build the trust over time. "We came out of Kah-Nee-Ta with some basic trust. It started there. People had a good feeling about that meeting. Those that were there recognized it wasn't going to be easy," Shively said. "You have to build trust, and that takes time. Ultimately, that was accomplished as a result of taking the attorneys out of the core discussions because they often aren't useful in this kind of process."

One of the thorniest issues taken up in the sessions was how to define "net" and "gross" revenues. A strict reading of ANCSA might have suggested a sharing of 70 percent of a corporation's gross resource revenues, which would have made development nearly impossible. Another point of dispute was how much to include in expenses that could be subtracted from gross revenues to get a net figure, especially how to determine overhead expenses.

John Schaeffer and Robert Newlin stand at the site of the world's largest and richest zinc deposit well before development of the mine began.

NANA Regional Corp. photo

Byron Mallott and Roy Huhndorf sign the historic 7(i) revenue-sharing agreement as Special Master Ralph Wienshienk looks on.

CIRI photo

"We agreed that it was net revenues that were to be shared, and we ultimately ended up with a formula for overhead expenses that was critical to our success. Without these decisions, there could have been endless audits and even lawsuits," Shively said.

The agreement was signed at CIRI offices on June 29, 1982. The agreement itself is 121 pages long, including 15 pages of definitions of terms such as "ANCSA lands," "surface rights," "fair market value," and others. It addresses all of the issues discussed in the year-long discussions.

After its adoption by the corporation leaders, it was turned over to the courts, accompanied by Wienschienk's 37-page report. These documents were approved by the court and form the basis for the dismissal in 1983 of the key lawsuit pending at the time, Aleut Corp. V. Arctic Slope Regional Corp.

Today, the agreement has become "standard operating procedure" for all Native corporations. Millions of dollars in checks have been exchanged. In fact, since ANCSA's passage in 1971, nearly $675 million has been shared. The two corporations sharing the most revenue over the years have been Sealaska and CIRI. Third highest in sharing is Arctic Slope Regional Corp.

"We don't even think about it any more, except how much do we have to give away this year," said Oliver Leavitt, former ASRC Board chairman. "We're resigned to the law and we abide by it."

Carl Marrs, former President and CEO of CIRI, believes that 7(i) is a powerful mechanism for the redistribution of wealth. Marrs believes that the revenue sharing provision of ANCSA may be a model for Lower 48 Indians and possibly indigenous people in other parts of the world. He suggests, for example, that a portion of gambling revenues from casinos operated by tribes could be shared among all Lower 48 tribes because the success of one casino over another is often due largely to its location.

One legal scholar has suggested that the sharing provisions of ANCSA made its passage possible and has also suggested its possible application in the Lower 48: "Although this was not articulated in House and Senate reports or within the hearings, Alaska Natives may have been able to negotiate the management of their own resources because of this revenue-sharing provision. Lucky groups, in effect, became the trustee of the unlucky groups. American Indian tribes could negotiate the same arrangements. The trust relationship could be ended, the price being capital to develop resources and an obligation to share revenues from that development," according to Sarah Arnott.

Seven(i) does not have unanimous support among Alaska Native leaders today. When interviewed by the *Alaska Business Monthly* magazine in the spring of 2002, Sealaska's President and CEO Chris McNeil Jr. pointed out that Sealaska had contributed significantly to the success of all Native corporations as a result of its 7(i) payments over the three decades of ANCSA. And he lamented what might have been, had Sealaska not been required by the sharing requirement.

"But sometimes I think about how much further we could have gone as a corporation if we didn't have to manage our business investments and the requirements of the 7(i) agreement among all ANCSA regional corporations," McNeil said. McNeil's predecessor Robert Loescher went even further in his earlier criticism of the sharing provision, calling it "anti-capitalistic."

"No other corporations in America have to revenue share on the basis the Alaska Native corporations have to. It puts a large burden of risk on the corporations to develop these resources and then they have to share their revenues with the other regions that do not have to share the same risk."

There are also concerns about how the agreement affects Native regional corporation business decisions. Jim Mery, vice president of lands and resources for Doyon, Ltd.

believes that requiring corporations to share 70 percent of their resource revenues with others makes undertaking development on Native land difficult. He says it's a virtually insurmountable constraint when it comes to development without a partner.

"I blow hot and cold on the 7(i) provision. There is a bit of fairness and

Sen. Henry M. "Scoop" Jackson
Henry M. Jackson Foundation photo

December 16, 1981 – Senator commemorates claims act anniversary

On Dec. 16, 1981, Sen. Henry M. Jackson, a key architect of the Alaska Native Claims Settlement Act of 1971, commemorated the act's anniversary in a speech to the Alaska Federation of Natives in Anchorage.

Jackson recalled that when efforts to settle Native land claims began in earnest in 1968, early proposals called only for small acreages around villages and cash payments totaling about $20 million. Jackson, a Democrat from Washington who served in Congress for nearly 43 years, said that "hard, careful work" by the Native leadership led to final version of the act, in which Alaska Natives retained 44 million acres and were granted nearly $1 billion.

Jackson was born in Everett, Wash., in 1912 and died there in 1983 at the age of 71. Known as "Scoop" Jackson, he won his first election to the U.S. House of Representatives in 1940 and was re-elected five times. He began his more than 30-year career in the Senate after his election in 1952.

Jackson played a pivotal role in the development and passage of ANCSA, which he referred to as "a bold, radical and totally untested experiment in government, in social ordering, and in private enterprise."

Unlike treaties with Indians in the Lower 48, ANCSA transferred land and cash to business enterprises, vesting control for the assets in the hands of Native people themselves. In his 1981 speech, Jackson discussed the inherent tension in the "ANCSA experiment," pointing out widespread debate over whether Native corporations should be operated with a focus on the "bottomline" or whether they should be operated to achieve social welfare and community objectives.

"This is a debate which I have watched for the past 13 years. It is a debate for which there are no ultimate answers. At one time, I thought it was a serious mistake to mix social welfare objectives with the traditional corporation's more limited objective of maximizing profitability," he said. "Today, I must confess to having changed my mind. The regional corporations are totally unique. Their performance cannot be measured by gross revenue and net profit standards alone. Judgments about their performance must be made on the basis of total performance in the achievement of shareholder goals."

- December 21, 2003

nobility about sharing everything," said Mery who served as Doyon's chief counsel before assuming his current position. He added that the revenue stream has propped up a number of the smaller village corporations that might otherwise have gone bankrupt. At the same time, there is no incentive for a region to develop its own resources in an active role; regions are almost forced into a passive position with a partner taking on most of the risk, he noted.

Another problem Mery points to is that the further people get away from the agreement, the harder it is to remember why particular provisions are in it. "There are fewer people who understand this than there used to be," he said.

The complexities of the agreement as well as the sharing requirement itself act as disincentives to look for resources on corporation lands, Mery said. On the other hand, he said Doyon has learned to live within the constraints. And it may be that keeping corporations from active development, which has such huge risks, is not all bad, he added.

"It hasn't impeded us from taking a passive role," he said. "We're getting other people to spend their money looking for things on our land. It hasn't hurt is in that regard," he said. "Exploration is a very risky venture. Should we be there anyway?"

Mery said another concern about the agreement is the fact that it can be changed only with the approval of all 12 regions. Over the years, he noted, Doyon has made proposals for modest changes, none of which have been adopted. "How do you get 12 regions to the table?" he asked.

There are numerous other controversies surrounding the implementation of Section 7(i) and sharing. Over the years, critics have raised concerns about what they believe is ASRC's reticence to share. They cite the fact that the corporation got subsurface land within the Arctic National Wildlife Refuge through a complex land trade with the federal government that will exempt the corporation from sharing. If oil development takes place in ANWR and significant deposits of oil are discovered, ASRC will not be required to share its revenues because the corporation traded surface land elsewhere for subsurface estate near Kaktovik in ANWR. Many different land trade scenarios are addressed in the 7(i) agreement, and surface/subsurface trades are specifically exempted from 7(i) sharing.

Leavitt said ASRC has long had concerns about 7(i) and that corporation leaders often wish sharing wasn't required. He said in the early days of lobbying for ANCSA, ASRC leadership sought to set the level for sharing at 50 percent or less, as opposed to 70 percent. He explained that because the huge Prudhoe Bay oilfield was discovered within the Inupiat people's traditional territory and yet went to the State of Alaska, there has long been a concern that the rightful land owners have been left out. "We fought pretty hard, but we lost. There didn't seem to be much sympathy for us," he said.

On the other hand, he said that ASRC recognizes "that's history" and tries to live within the requirements of the law and the agreement. Leavitt noted that during the formulation of the 7(i) agreement, it became apparent to the ASRC leadership that there was support among all the corporations for exempting surface/subsurface land trades from 7(i). Early on, ASRC leadership decided if they could structure a land trade with the federal government and obtain subsurface lands around Kaktovik, they would be exempted from 7(i), he said.

"We played by the rules," said Jake Adams, ASRC President & CEO.

Additionally, both Leavitt and Adams noted that other oil deposits on ASRC lands, such as the Alpine discovery, are sharable under Section 7(i). "With the Alpine oil field, we're probably giving away $20 million a year out of our bottom line, and it will go on for a long time. It may even increase," Leavitt said.

ASRC may be one of the biggest contributors to 7(i) sharing in the future, and both Leavitt and Adams say they have philosophical questions about it. "When we catch a whale, we share it with our fellow Eskimos," Leavitt said, not with Athabascans or Tlingits or other Alaska Native cultures. And what is traditionally shared is the whale and other subsistence wildlife resources, not the cash that is part of the Western world.

October 11, 1982 – NANA, Cominco sign Red Dog pact

The Red Dog Mine in Northwestern Alaska, at the site of the world's largest and richest zinc deposit, can date one of its key milestones to the mining lease agreement signed on October 11, 1982, by NANA Regional Corp., the Alaska Native regional corporation headquartered in Kotzebue, and Cominco, the Canadian mining company now called Teck Cominco.

The agreement, which led to the opening of the mine in 1989, authorizes Teck Cominco to mine and sell minerals and requires it to pay royalties to NANA, which in turn distributes 70 percent of its net revenue among all 12 instate Native regional corporations as required under the sharing provisions of the Alaska Native Claims Settlement Act. Between 1982 and 2003, NANA received $79.2 million in royalties. The total annual mine payroll is $45.5 million.

Prior to 1982, the NANA board spent six years meeting in the region's 11 villages to discuss issues related to mining. While many of the region's residents favored job creation and economic growth, they stressed repeatedly that protection of subsistence and the land came first.

One result of these concerns was that the mine's Subsistence Advisory Committee, including eight NANA shareholders from the neighboring villages of Kivalina and Noatak, was created to monitor the environmental impacts of the mine and its effects on subsistence resources. Even so, claims of air and water quality regulatory violations have led to the state and federal government both levying fines. In addition, six Kivalina villagers represented by a California environmental public interest law firm have filed a citizens' suit against Teck Cominco, alleging violations of the Clean Water Act.

Two of the key NANA leaders responsible for

the agreement were John Schaeffer, former NANA president, and Robert Newlin, past chairman of the NANA board. They were joint recipients of the 1986 NANA Shareholder of the Year Award, and their respect for each other was reflected in their acceptance speeches.

"I could not have done anything without Robert. I want to thank you for putting me in the same place as Robert, the greatest honor you could give me," Schaeffer said. Newlin said: "I do not deserve it; it was done by John, the board, the staff, and mostly my wife."

- October 10, 2004

"I blow hot and cold on the 7(i) provision. There is a bit of fairness and nobility about sharing everything."

— Jim Mery, 2002

"It's hard for us to say we like it (the sharing provision). Nobody in America does that. Even the other tribes never did that in the Lower 48. When it comes to money, it's American, Western society – they still expect us to do the things major corporations do," Leavitt said.

Adams said that many of ASRC's business partners, as well as most non-Natives throughout Alaska do not understand that ASRC and any resource-rich Alaska Native Corporation is required to give away 70 percent of its resource revenues.

On the other hand, neither has any plans to seek the congressional action that would be required to eliminate 7(i), in part because of the bad blood it would create among other Alaska Native Corporations. But they also believe that failure to resolve the 7(i) conflicts years ago could have been the downfall of ANCSA and that the 7(i) agreement and its implementation is a remarkable story.

"I'm just glad it's behind us. It's something that was tearing us apart, even good friends," Leavitt said.

It may be that 7(i)'s unique sharing requirement is truly a double-edged sword. The "haves" are forced to help the "have-nots." Significantly, this sharing has been accomplished through an agreement that Native leaders themselves crafted. It took all of the leaders from each of the regions countless hours over a period of months – often personal time away from families and their other professional commitments – to hammer out the agreement. And they were the only ones who could achieve a settlement. It was, in fact, an achievement that many said was impossible. Left to advocates who tenaciously hung on only to their client's interests without taking into account the broad needs of the entire Alaska Native community, it probably would have been an insurmountable problem.

The Native leadership was able to look at the broader picture in crafting the agreement. While the leaders understood the costs would be heavy for the corporations that were "haves," they also understood the immense benefits for the "have-nots." In the end, it was apparent to most observers that neither the courts nor the attorneys the corporations hired could solve the 7(i) disputes. Only the Native leadership coming together to work for the greater good of the entire Native Community could seize the initiative and solve the problem.

A new kind of Native sharing provides steady stream of revenue to villages

A unique aspect of the Alaska Native Claims Settlement Act sharing provisions is the creation of a steady stream of revenue for village corporations, as well as individual Native shareholders who are shareholders only of a regional corporation and not a village corporation, known as "at-large" shareholders.

"For some village corporations, it's the only income," said Tom Hawkins, Chief Operating Officer of Bristol Bay Native Corporation and the former chief executive officer of Choggiung, Ltd., the village corporation formed by the merger of village corporations for Dillingham, Ekuk and Portage Creek in the Bristol Bay Region. "Getting the 7(i) check is a big deal."

Section 7(j) of the Alaska Native Claims Settlement Act calls for half of the resource funds received by each Native regional corporation to be distributed to the villages within the region and at-large shareholders. The amounts distributed annually are determined by a formula based on population.

Hawkins noted that there are 22 villages in the region and that most have a very small population. He pointed out that 17 of the Bristol Bay villages are in the Lake and Peninsula Borough, which has a total population of about 1,700 people.

Choggiung, Ltd., is the largest of the Bristol Bay village corporations, and its share of the 7(j) funds is about 20 percent of the total Bristol Bay distributes to villages. Choggiung's checks have been averaging about $150,000 a year in recent years. Hawkins said that's a significant amount of money each year, especially since it's essentially a windfall. "All you have to do is cash it," he said.

Eben Hopson
Hopson family photo

November 7, 1922 – Birth of Eben Hopson

Inupiaq leader Eben Hopson, Sr., was born in Barrow on Nov. 7, 1922. The founding mayor of the North Slope Borough and a lifelong whaler, Hopson spent his life fighting for the Inupiaq people.

His parents were Al and Maggie Hopson, and his paternal grandfather was Fred Hopson, a whaler from Liverpool, England, who settled in Barrow in 1886.

Hopson served in the Army in World War II and returned home to Barrow after the war, and he and his wife Rebecca (Panigeo) together raised a family that included 12 children.

Hopson entered politics as a member of the Barrow City Council in 1946. He was elected to the Alaska Territorial Legislature in 1956, and after Statehood, he was elected to the first State Senate. Hopson was the first executive director of the Arctic Slope Native Association, which he helped organize in 1965. In 1968, he moved to Anchorage to become the executive director of the Alaska Federation of Natives.

Hopson left AFN to become special assistant for Native Affairs to Governor William A. Egan in 1970. His dream was to encourage the development of local government in rural Alaska, culminating in 1972 in the creation of the North Slope

Borough, encompassing an area about the size of Minnesota.

Hopson also hoped to unite the Native people of the world's northern regions, and in 1976, he called together Inuit leaders of Greenland, Canada, the United States and the USSR to form the Inuit Circumpolar Conference.

Speaking before the ICC General Assembly in 1992, Hopson's daughter Flossie Hopson Andersen offered this eulogy: "I would like to tell you first who my father was. Eben Hopson was a politician and a statesman. He was a man with a vision of life and the future unlike any other. Above all else, he was a true Inupiaq leader. " Hopson died June 28, 1980, when he was 57. A biography is included in the book, "Taking Control, The North Slope Borough, the Story of Self-Determination in the Arctic," by Bill Hess and published in 1993 by the North Slope Borough.

- November 9, 2003

"I'm just glad it's behind us. It's something that was tearing us apart, even good friends."

— Oliver Leavitt, 2002

Judy Nelson, another former CEO of Choggiung who served in that capacity for 11 years, said for a number of years, the 7(i) money was one of the village corporation's chief sources of revenue. Nelson said that the corporation has always been conservative in its approach to investing and has always been solvent. Still, the steady stream of 7(j) money was welcome. And she added that revenue-sharing funds weren't just a welcome windfall for villages that struggled financially, but a critical source of revenue. Nelson said in Choggiung's case, the checks "helped to make the corporation grow."

Karl Potts, also a former Choggiung Chief Executive Officer, said that over time, the 7(i) revenue has gradually become less significant as the corporation's consolidated income has increased. The corporation's consolidated income for 1999 was nearly $9.7 million, compared to nearly $10.6 million for 2000 and about $18.6 million for 2001. The 7(i) portion of the income for those three years was $136,637 for 1999, $159,232 for 2000 and $159,732 for 2001.

Potts said that early in Choggiung's history, the annual 7(i) revenues were extremely important in allowing the company to operate profitably.

"Prior to 1993, the 7(i) component of Choggiung's financial performance represented a substantial percentage of total revenues. Over the past 10 years, the proportional impact of 7(i) revenues has declined as Choggiung's businesses have matured and grown. Notwithstanding this fact, 7(i) participation will continue to be a significant component of Choggiung's financial structure. It is indeed, one of the most prominent aspects of ANCSA which embodies a united culture of sharing natural resources for the benefit of the larger community of Alaska Natives. In today's competitive business environment, such opportunities are rare indeed."

Special Master praises Native agreement on 7(i)

The sharing agreement hammered out by the regions in the early 1980s is a remarkable achievement, especially when viewed by Western standards. In order to reach the agreement, Native leaders had to set aside their individual corporate agendas and focus on the well-being of the entire Native Community as a whole.

It was upheld on March 28, 1983, when Special Master Ralph Wienshienk issued his assessment, calling it "fair and feasible and in the best interests of the Regional Corporations and the Native community of Alaska." Wienshienk's report stated that the agreement meets these standards because:

- The agreement establishes a system of accounting and reporting that resolves the issues of the pending litigation, reduces the likelihood of future litigation, enables each Regional Corporation to plan for the future and, being uniform, makes the accounting of each Regional Corporation comparable and understandable to the others;

- The agreement adopts and codifies the Court's broad interpretation of what constitutes 7(i) Revenues and thus accomplishes the Congressional mandate that resource wealth be equitably distributed.

- The Agreement defines all expenses which are a prerequisite to or consequence of the production of 7(i) Revenues and, whenever possible in order to minimize future disagreements, substitutes reasonable conventions and standards for generally accepted accounting principles which are subjective in their application.

Vicki Otte, left, and Barbara Donatelli are shown in this mid-1980s photo in Nicolai.

Vicki Otte photo

October 29, 1976 – Four villages merge to form MTNT

On Oct. 29, 1976, the 333 shareholders of four Interior Alaska villages in the Doyon Region disbanded their individual village corporations and merged to form MTNT, Ltd. The name is taken from the initials of the four villages McGrath, Nikolai, Takotna and Telida.

Vicki Otte, who served on the nine-member board for 20 years beginning in 1983, said the merger was undertaken so that the village corporations could pool their resources. Although MTNT has experienced ups and downs over the years, Otte said there is no question that merging was the right decision.

Throughout the years, MTNT has invested in ventures such as the local electric utility, a construction company, tourism and real estate. When MTNT bought Kodiak Auto Center in Kodiak, it became the first Native-owned auto dealership in the country in 1998. In recent years, MTNT has divested itself of some of its less successful business ventures, including the auto dealership. Its leading subsidiary today is Sentinel Industries, which focuses on government contracts. Last year, Sentinel accounted for $33 million of the company's $40 million in revenue.

Otte said the corporation is focusing on increasing its net revenues and has trimmed its overhead by eliminating several positions. The company is now managed by Bob Coghill, formerly of Nenana, who is now based in McGrath. Previously, the corporation's top managers lived in Anchorage.

MTNT has paid out annual dividends for years, ranging from about $200 to $1,000. Since 1987, dividends have been funded through the earnings of the corporation's permanent fund, which today has investments totaling nearly $1.5 million. For many years, the corporation has funded scholarships for shareholders and their families.

The merged corporation has a large land base of nearly 300,000 acres, most of which remains undeveloped. As a village corporation, the company controls only the surface estate. The subsurface estate is owned by the Native regional corporation, Doyon, Ltd.

Each year, the corporation's annual report features one of the shareholder elders on its cover. Shareholder Ann Demientieff of McGrath was featured on the Fiscal Year 2003 report.

- November 7, 2004

- The Agreement's provisions serve to advance resource development while also encouraging economy and efficiency to protect revenues from waste.

- The Agreement provides mechanisms for compliance and dispute resolution that operate to minimize the potential for future litigation.

6. 1991 Amendments make ANCSA more "Native"

Amendments to the Alaska Native Claims Settlement Act passed in 1988 were a radical shift for the act. The sweeping "1991" amendments to ANCSA continued restrictions on the sale of Native corporation stock unless a majority of the shareholders voted in favor of ending them.

It was not at all clear when ANCSA was passed in 1971 that shareholders would ever get such an opportunity. And even as recently as the mid-1980's when the "1991" amendments were under consideration in Congress, the choice on the continuation of Native control was not a foregone conclusion.

Ramsey Clark addresses the Alaska Federation of Natives Convention, focusing on the 1991 issue of whether restrictions on the sale of Native corporation stock should have been lifted 20 years after passage of the Alaska Natives Claims Settlement Act of 1971.

Tundra Times photo

ANCSA's passage in 1971 was the result of work by people with many different agendas. There was a wide gulf between those who wanted to impose a Western value system on Alaska's First People and many of the Native people themselves who were trying to craft a creative alternative to the reservation system in the Lower 48 which yoked people to the hulking bureaucracy of the Bureau of Indian Affairs.

Joseph H. Fitzgerald, former chairman of the Federal Field Committee, which developed a massive landmark publication that detailed the plight of Alaska Natives in 1968, favored settling land claims. But Fitzgerald's view

July 24, 1983 – ICC announces Berger to head Native inquiry

On the eve of the opening of the Inuit Circumpolar Conference at Frobisher Bay – July 24, 1983 – ICC Executive Committee member James Stotts of Barrow announced that Canadian Supreme Court Justice Thomas R. Berger had been selected to chair a commission to study the impacts of the Alaska Native Claims Settlement Act of 1971. Berger, one of Canada's foremost advocates of Native rights, had earlier been appointed by the Canadian government to conduct the Mackenzie Valley Pipeline Inquiry.

The ANCSA study was called the Alaska Native Review Commission. It was sponsored by the ICC and the World Council of Indigenous Peoples.

"This was the first time that anybody outside of ANCSA had taken a look at its implementation," said attorney David Case, who served as counsel to the Berger commission. Berger held hearings over a period of about 18 months in 62 villages throughout Alaska, drawing testimony from hundreds of Alaska Natives. Also invited to comment on the dramatic impact of ANCSA were indigenous people from throughout the world. "He didn't commission a bunch of experts to write a report. His process was to go to villages, open up the microphone and listen to the people," Case said.

Vernita Herdman, former advocacy coordinator at the Rural Alaska Community Action Program, said the first time she went to a roundtable discussion on Feb. 27, 1984, in Anchorage, held as part of the study, "I was immediately enthralled."

Herdman said Berger's study and his ensuing book, "Village Journey," did much to further her understanding of the important role tribes play in Alaska and their tribal sovereignty. "People were worried about their ability to retain the land and many other issues. Berger validated what our tribal leaders were saying, which was not that ANCSA was wrong, but that it was not comprehensive," Herdman said.

On a statewide level, many observers believe that Berger's book sparked spirited debate and helped lead to the passage of amendments to ANCSA allowing shareholders of Native corporations to continue restrictions on stock sales and retain their Native ownership.

- July 27, 2003

Janie Leask, joined at an Anchorage hearing in the mid-1980's by John Shively, presents testimony concerning the 1991 issue.
Tundra Times photo

of the creation of corporations can only be seen as a type of termination. Restrictions on the sale of stock would end 10 years after passage of the law, under a proposal he offered.

"Each Native may hold his stock or sell it as he desires, and you or I may buy stock if we desire without racial restrictions. In short, 'aboriginal rights' are to be exchanged for useful and relevant civil rights," he testified in 1969.

At the other end of the spectrum were Alaska Natives whose urgent task in the face of the State of Alaska beginning its selection of 104 million acres of land, was to protect as much land as they could and make sure that it remained under Native control. In the end, they settled for a 20-year moratorium on stock sales. Twenty years seemed like a long way into the future, and those who were concerned about it felt that it was enough time to craft whatever changes were needed.

Thomas R. Berger spent 18 months traveling to 62 villages throughout Alaska to gather information on the Alaska Native Claims Settlement Act.
Bill Hess photo

Byron Mallott, former CEO of Sealaska Corporation and one of the architects of ANCSA, says what gives him hope about ANCSA despite his misgivings over some of its features is that it has been very much a living document.

"We've been able to amend it as time, circumstance and policy requirements have required. And one of the most critical of those changes has been the change in the 20-year prohibition on the sale of stock," he said. "I think that there was a recognition among policy makers and the general public that this made sense, that these corporations did belong to Alaska Natives and that they should make decisions as to their future, as to whether their stock was alienable or not."

Hjalmar E. Olson has been a leader in the Bristol Region for many years and has been a director of BBNC since 1974.

Tundra Times photo

Bristol Bay becomes an advocate for Native stock ownership

The "1991 amendments" to the Alaska Native Claims Settlement Act contained special provisions sought by Bristol Bay Native Corp. that were there because corporation officials listened to legal advice — and not their own people.

But within a year, BBNC recognized its error and successfully lobbied Congress — with the blessing of the Alaska Federation of Natives — to allow the corporation to remain a Native-

Calista leader dies Dec. 11, 1987

When Edward "Eddie" Hoffman Sr. died Dec. 11, 1987, at age 70, he was unquestionably one of the most outspoken champions of the Yukon-Kuskokwim Delta Region and one of the area's key leaders. A few lines from a poem written by Sue Gamache, vice president/shareholder services for Calista Corp., offer insight into his style:

Hail to the Chief,
who told it to us straight.
You bawled us out and gave us hell
but deep inside, we knew you meant well.
You were always there to lend a hand,
to fight a cause or save our land.

"Those who knew him on a personal level recall his generosity, in particular his fondness for Elders and young children. It was very fitting that the City of Bethel renamed the Bethel Senior Center, the Eddie Hoffman Senior Center in memory of the chief," Gamache said.

Hoffman was born April 9, 1917, in Napaimiut, the seventh of 12 children born to George Hoffman Sr. and Elizabeth Lind. He lived most of his life in Bethel, where he served at different times as mayor, president of the Bethel Native Corp. and a director of Calista Corp. He and Bessie Chief were married on January 6, 1941, and had three daughters and five sons. He purchased a fuel truck in the late 1950's and began operating as Hoffman Fuel Service, but he continued to participate in the subsistence and commercial fisheries in the region.

The *Tundra Drums* of Bethel covered Hoffman's death in its Dec. 17, 1987, issue with the headline: Our Chief is Gone. The obituary printed by the paper recounted a number of stories about Hoffman, including one that illustrated his critical view of bureaucracy. According to the paper: "Soon after the power plant burned down in the mid-1970's, the top military brass arrived in Bethel to 'ascertain the power needs of the city and fuel needs of the surrounding villages.' After listening to what Eddie considered to be pompous pronouncements about how this information was to be gathered, Eddie stood up, pointed his finger at the top, top brass and bellowed, 'You, you stupid!!'"

Hoffman was one of the founders of the Association of Village Council Presidents, a non-profit organization of 57 Southwest Alaska villages. AVCP bestowed on him the lifetime title of Traditional Chief of AVCP.

- December 16, 2001

May 1, 1994 – Report outlines stark problems

The Alaska Natives Commission on May 1, 1994, issued its three-volume report on the status of Alaska Natives. The commission's work was concentrated over the course of about 18 months and included gathering data and testimony from throughout the state. The report stated that it "paints a picture of 86,000 U.S. citizens living in the richest state of the union who, despite such fortunate geographic placement, have experienced – and are today experiencing – economic deprivation and social impairment at sometimes incomprehensible rates." It blamed a "systematic assumption of responsibility and control by outsiders" as the "fundamental fact underlying the contemporary Native social and economic crisis."

controlled corporation beyond the 1991 cutoff.

The issue is complex and more than a little confusing, but for Trefon Angasan, former BBNC Vice President of Shareholder Relations, it boils down to a simple case of Native leaders listening to legal advice at the expense of their own people.

"We plowed a lot of resources into trying to preserve the opportunity for stock to become alienable after 1991. And our advice was legal advice, purely legal," Angasan said. "We left out the emotional issues, the ties to the communities."

Many Alaska Native leaders in the early 1980's were trying to address what to do in 1991 when stock would become alienable under ANCA's provisions as the act was passed in 1971. Under AFN's leadership, they spent several years lobbying Congress to authorize continued restrictions on stock sales after 1991. According to amendments passed in 1988, the only way the restrictions can be lifted is for shareholders to petition the corporation, which is then obligated to carry out a vote, allowing the shareholders to decide whether they want to lift restrictions.

That concept did not sit well with BBNC, however, and corporation officials were successful in getting provisions included calling for BBNC stock to become alienable unless shareholders voted otherwise.

"We got the law passed, then we began to think about what we did," Angasan said. "We began to listen to the hue and cry of the Native community and how they were very persistent, very determined to continue stock restrictions. And when we listened to that, we began to wonder about the land that the settlement act provided for us," he said. The thought that non-Natives could eventually gain control of BBNC and then its lands sent corporate leadership back to the shareholders for meetings to discuss the issue.

"It was a mistake, and we acknowledged it," he said. Angasan said BBNC's turnaround is probably unprecedented in the Native community, including their success in getting their provisions passed and then repealed. "We've gone the extra mile at both ends of the spectrum. Now we are the strongest advocates for stock restrictions."

As a result of the stormy discussions, Angasan said BBNC did a lot of soul-searching and eventually reorganized its operations, revamping the land department and becoming more service-oriented.

"I think we've learned from that," he said. "We've become better leaders. We've become more sensitive to the culture of our people. We've become more sensitive to their needs."

Congressional action to create the commission came in 1989, a year after the *Anchorage Daily News* published its stunning Pulitzer-prize winning series on Alaska Natives called "A People in Peril." Also shedding light on Native problems was a report published by the Alaska Federation of Natives, "A Call to Action."

The commission's staff was led by Mike Irwin, who today works for AFN and is also serving as chairman of Doyon, Ltd. Co-chairs of the commission were Perry Eaton and Mary Jane Fate. Other commissioners included Johne Binkley, the late Edgar Paul Boyko, Father Norman H.V. Elliott, Beverly Masek, Martin B. Moore Sr., Frank Pagano, John Schaeffer, Father James A. Sebesta, Walter A. Soboleff, the late Morris Thompson and Sam Towarak. Francis E. Hamilton of Ketchikan served on the commission until her death in 1992.

In order to gather information, the commission held nine regional hearings between July 1992 and October 1993 in Fairbanks, Bethel, Nome, Klawock, Barrow, Dillingham, Kodiak, Kotzebue and Copper Center. In addition, the commission's four task forces held hearings in Fort Yukon, Emmonak, Alakanuk, Hooper Bay, Anchorage, Eagle River, Kenai, Sitka and Angoon.

- May 5, 2002

7. Subsistence is what connects you to the seasons and the land

By Trefon Angasan

Trefon Angasan
BBNC photo

I started to write about subsistence with the notion that there was a clear vision by the Alaska Native People on how to resolve the subsistence issue. However, I now realize that the Native People do not agree on this complex and wrenching issue. Although the Alaska Supreme Court made a devastating decision to strike down the state subsistence law in 1989, there appeared to be no sense of urgency because Alaska Natives have always believed the federal government would protect subsistence, or that eventually the state would come through. But when I began to do my research, I learned that statewide organizations representing Native interests had a different view of the way that the subsistence issue would be resolved. I hope to show that there is precedence in federal law to give the Alaska Native Peoples the protections that they need. In fact, I believe federal law is the only avenue that will provide a final solution to the Alaska Natives' subsistence dilemma.

Something very important to the conscience of America is happening in Alaska as we enter a new century. Most citizens of the United States have never heard of it, but it involves the most divisive and dangerous issue in the politics of Alaska, the largest state by far in the United States. The way in which it is resolved will have a greater impact on the future of all Alaskans than any other public policy question. On the larger scale of history, it will tell us whether Americans have learned anything from the country's great mistakes.

As used in modern Alaska, the word "subsistence" means the hunting, fishing and gathering activities that have provided food to Alaska's Native People for more than 10,000 years. These practices continue to flourish in most areas of the state today.

Before the arrival of the non-Natives, subsistence was the only form of economic production by which the aboriginal populations fed, clothed, and housed themselves. Conducted in seasonal cycles by semi-nomadic bands within recognized territories, subsistence led to the development of traditional, small-scale technologies for harvesting and preserving foods, and it distributed the resulting production through a communal network of sharing and bartering.

Subsistence provides life in many ways. If you are an Alaska Native, it tells you who you are, what you are worth and who loves you. It assigns roles by gender and age. It obliges you to work with others. When you are old, it guarantees that others will provide for you. The language of your ancestors, with all those words for different kinds of snow, is built on it. Subsistence is what connects you to the seasons and the land.

In 1989, the Alaska Supreme Court struck down the state law that complied with Alaska National Interest Lands Conservation Act of 1980 that provided a rural priority for subsistence users. The court ruled that the law was unconstitutional. The governor, with support from the Native Community, offered a constitutional amendment restoring a subsistence priority, but that plan has been repeatedly rejected by the state legislature.

For thousands of years, Alaska Native people have survived by living from Alaska's land and waters. Hunting, fishing and gathering constitutes the spiritual, medicinal, nutritional and cultural foundation of Alaska's indigenous peoples and the Native village cultures.

To most Americans, the vast stretches of forest, tundra, and mountain lands in Alaska constitute a wilderness in the most absolute sense of the word. In their minds, the land is wilderness because it is undisturbed, pristine, and lacking in obvious signs of human activity. To Americans, undisturbed land is unoccupied or unused land. However, most of Alaska is not wilderness in this sense of the word, nor has it been for thousands of years. Much of Alaska's apparently untrodden forest and tundra land is thoroughly known by people whose entire lives and cultural ancestry is intimately associated with it. Indeed, to the Native inhabitants, these lands are no more an unknown wilderness than are the streets of a city to its residents. The fact that the American people identify Alaska's remote country derives from their inability to conceive of occupying and utilizing land without altering or completely eliminating its natural state. But the Alaska Natives have been living this way for thousands of years. They have successfully participated in their ecosystem. This represents an exemplary form of human adaptation, fostering a healthy coexistence of man and ecosystem.

The Solicitor's Office in the Department Interior set down the legal basis for the protection of the Alaska Native fishing rights in a 1937 opinion in response to certain questions of the Indian Office. The opinion stated that the reservation authority of the Secretary of the Interior under the 1936 Alaska Act included the authority to reserve submerged lands actually occupied by Alaska Natives. The question of this new authority was upheld by the U.S. Supreme Court in Hynes v. Grimes in 1949. In December 1937, the National Resources Committee published a regional planning report on Alaska which indicated that the Department of Interior had under consideration the establishment of fishing reservations in Alaska under the Indian Reorganization Act (formerly known as the Wheeler-Howard Act). This effort was stymied by the Seattle-owned canning industry who feared that they would lose the ability to harvest the great runs of salmon in Southeast Alaska.

As for protections offered to the Native People on game, the Alaska Game Law of 1925 was believed to provide the most for subsistence hunting during territorial days. The law stated that ". . .any Indian or Eskimo, prospector, or travelers (can) take animals, birds, or game fishes during the closed season when he is in the need for food."

In 1959, the Alaska Statehood Act gave the new State of Alaska the right to regulate hunting and fishing for all Alaskans, including Natives.

The Alaska Federation of Natives was the first statewide Native organization to seek protections for subsistence for Native people. AFN leadership testified in support of subsistence protections in 1968 at the first congressional hearings held on Alaska Native land claims. At that time, Emil Notti, the president of the AFN testified: "the Native People of Alaska are facing a daily crisis just to survive and the situation is getting worse as Alaska develops and grows in population. Unless relief is forthcoming, it is conceivable that we may face starvation in the most affluent country in the world."

In spite of the pleading by the AFN in 1968, Congress in 1971 passed the Alaska Native Claims Settlement Act to settle Alaska Natives' aboriginal land claims and in granting land and cash to Alaska Natives, extinguished aboriginal hunting and fishing rights. At the same time, Congress mandated that the State of Alaska and the U.S. Secretary of the Interior protect Native subsistence rights.

In 1980, Congress passed the Alaska National Interest Lands Conservation Act, known as ANILCA. Title VIII of the act was adopted because the State of Alaska and the U.S. Department of Interior were not protecting Native subsistence in rural villages. The Act stated that "on all federal lands and reserved waters in Alaska, rural residents would have a priority for subsistence fishing and hunting." The State was offered the right to manage subsistence on all Alaska lands and waters if it would enact a state law giving rural residents the same subsistence priority in state law. In 1982, the State's Boards of Fisheries and Game established regulations (5 AAC 99.010) specifying that customary and traditional uses are "rural" uses. As a result, the Department of Interior certified the State's consistency with ANILCA. The anti-subsistence lobby did not agree with the regulation and sponsored a statewide ballot initiative that called for repeal of the state law allowing for the rural preference. Ballot Proposition 7 was placed

"We're asking for 40 million acres and, of course, these millions of acres actually are ours. The only reason I am pushing for the bill is because this is all we could get at the present time. At the present time, we have no choice."

— State Senator Raymond C. Christiansen, 1968

on the ballot. A majority of the voters voted against the proposition (58.38 percent), demonstrating broad public support for subsistence.

In 1989, the Alaska Supreme Court, in a case brought by anti-subsistence groups, struck down the state's rural priority as a violation of the Alaska Constitution. Without such priority in state law, ANILCA required the federal government to assume management of subsistence on federal lands and waters. When the federal government took over the subsistence management on federal lands, it did so only for hunting on land, not for subsistence fishing on federal waters.

Natives had to sue the federal government to prove that the term "federal public lands" included waters. Katie John, an Athabascan Elder who fished for subsistence all of her life on a tributary of the Copper River, was restricted from harvesting for her subsistence fish by fishwheel by the Alaska Department of Fish and Game in 1985. The State Board of Fisheries banned the use of fishwheels at her traditional fishing site. The board issued regulations that required that the harvest for salmon be taken only by hook and line at her fish camp. The board then set aside a location that was less favorable for fishwheel harvesting. Katie John sued the Board of Fisheries in State Court. The court ruled in her favor and instructed the Board of Fisheries to promulgate regulations that would restore Katie John's traditional harvest by fishwheel and to establish bag and possession limits in accordance with subsistence regulations. Before the state could respond to the decision, the Alaska Supreme Court ruled in the McDowell case in 1989 that Alaska's subsistence law was unconstitutional. This decision negated the prior court ruling directing the Department of Fish and Game to reinstate a subsistence fishery by fishwheel on the Copper River.

In the wake of *McDowell v. State*, the Secretary of Interior implemented a subsistence management program for the public lands in Alaska. The Secretary's takeover of subsistence regulations on public lands excluded subsistence fishing on navigable waters. Katie John again sued, this time in Federal District Court. In *Katie John v. United States* she alleged that the federal subsistence program mandated by ANILCA had been unlawfully restricted by excluding from its coverage navigable waters where the United States owns interests. The State was later added as a defendant. A year later, on February 27, 1992, the State filed a complaint in *Alaska v. Babbitt* which alleged that the Secretary had asserted subsistence management jurisdiction over certain navigable and non-navigable waters belonging to the State. The district court filed a decision on March 30, 1994, granting partial summary judgment in favor of Katie John and AFN in both the *Katie John* and the *State v. Babbitt* cases. In the *John v. United States decision*, No.s A90-0480 &A92-0264-0 CV (HRH). Judge Holland ruled:

- ANILCA's rural preference applies to all marine and navigable waters of Alaska.
- Federal agencies have direct legal authority to regulate subsistence of federal public lands (including waters) during dual management.

Both the state and federal government appealed the decision for various reasons. The 9th Circuit Court of Appeals issued its ruling on Katie John v. United States that ANILCA's subsistence priority applies to waters where the United States has reserved water rights. The court further held that the federal agencies that administer the subsistence priority are responsible for identifying those waters where subsistence fisheries occur.

In spite of the legal victories, the Alaska Native people continued to face the threats to their subsistence way of life by the State of Alaska's legislative leadership and the State's conservative courts. In May 1995, the Alaska Supreme Court ruled in the Kenaitze v. State that the domicile factor in the subsistence fishery in state law was unconstitutional. In August of that same year, in the case of Totemoff v. State, the courts ruled that the federal subsistence law does not preempt non-conflicting state law. The courts ruled that ANILCA did not need to protect traditional means and methods of harvest by the subsistence user. The ruling also disagreed with the Katie John ruling that public lands include certain navigable waters. This argu-

April 20, 1995 – 9th Circuit rules in Katie John's favor

Alaska Natives won a big victory in the fight for subsistence rights on April 20, 1995, when the Ninth Circuit Court of Appeals issued an opinion in favor of Athabascan Elders Katie John and Doris Charles of Mentasta.

The 2-1 Ninth Circuit Court ruling stated that the subsistence priority applied to fisheries on navigable waters. The court noted that federal intervention was called for because state subsistence policies did not protect villagers as required under the Alaska National Interest Lands Conservation Act of 1980. Arguing on the other side of the issue were attorneys representing the State of Alaska, who claimed that a subsistence priority granted by the federal government applied only to navigable waters on federal land.

The taking of fish and game for subsistence purposes has been a hotly debated issue in Alaska for decades, and John's name has become emblematic of the debate. In 1964, the Alaska Board of Fisheries and Game shut down subsistence fishing at Batzulnetas, a former village that had become a seasonal fish camp in the Ahtna Region on the banks of the Copper River used by John and others. Later, John and others filed claims in the vicinity of the site, and in 1985 the Native American Rights Fund filed a suit on her behalf.

Throughout the years, the court and legislative battles have continued for John and other Alaska Natives throughout the state, as well as other rural Alaskans. Even today, a solution remains out of reach. A subsistence pamphlet prepared by the Alaska Federation of Natives notes that "three governors, eight regular legislative sessions, two special sessions and a host of actions by private interested have failed to resolve the impasse."

In the meantime, Alaska Natives continue to seek ways to protect their subsistence take of Alaska's wildlife resources. AFN's pamphlet states: "For many, subsistence defines what it means to be Alaskan — to live in harmony with nature and survive off the resources of the land and sea."

Asked how she feels about it, John says: "All we ever wanted was to catch fish."

- April 25, 2004

ment was presented to the U.S. Supreme Court on December 5, 1995. The Supreme Court denied the state's petition in May 1996.

In spite of the overwhelming problems imperiling Alaska Native societies, our cultures remain vibrant. Our languages and cultures have persisted, although changed, despite decades of governmental pressure to assimilate us into the larger society and the extensive forces of socio-cultural impacts impinging on our communities. We are among the last societies in North America who remain largely dependent and culturally attached to a hunting and gathering way of life. Today, many of us continue to practice ancient ceremonies and to hold the world view and values of our ancestors. For the United States, we represent a rich cultural resource that is worthy of protection.

The cultural component also includes ideologies and beliefs such as the recognition that wildlife has spirits and that Native people have kinship or special relationship with them. This relationship obliges Native people to adhere to certain codes of conduct and to treat animals in prescriptive ways to insure success in future hunts and to assure that animals will return to be harvest.

Katmai National Park and Preserve is located at the base of the Alaska Peninsula, a volcano-studded protrusion which stretches more than 400 miles to the southwest before it terminates at False Pass. An undeniably immense area is enclosed within the park. The lands and waters within its boundaries, 3,674,541 acres in Katmai National Park and another 418,699 acres in Katmai National Preserve, span almost the width of the peninsula. Its boundaries extend along the base of the peninsula in a north-south orientation for more than 100 miles. The present park and preserve is the fifth largest National Park Service unit in Alaska. Even so, the combined area of the two units is larger than Connecticut and Rhode Island put together; the areas are far more expansive than the largest national park in the Lower 48 and almost twice the size of Yellowstone. The Brooks Camp area of the Katmai has been a major focus of human activity for thousands of years and archaeologists have discovered scores of evidence of human occupation of the area's lakes, shores and coastline.

Hunting and fishing in the Katmai region has been traced back to prehistoric times, and during the historic period, trapping formed an integral part of the subsistence lifestyle of Katmai and other communities in the region. Some residents of Savonosky, a Katmai village, had a fish camp located at the Brooks River to take advantage of the remarkable salmon runs. Hunting, trapping and fishing patterns in the Katmai region were dramatically altered by one of the world's largest volcanic eruptions in recent history in June 1912.

In 1912, the residents of the Katmai Community evacuated to escape the volcanic eruption of Novarupta. The residents of the village of Savonoski fled to Naknek, located along the Naknek River on the Bristol Bay coast. They later settled six miles up the river from Naknek at a place that they named New Savonoski. The residents did not adapt well to the location. It was laden with swamp and lacked wood for firewood. They had to scavenge lumber from abandoned canneries along the coast of Bristol Bay to build new homes. They were plagued by mosquitoes. They tried to move back to their homeland but found it uninhabitable. Pelagia Melganek, the matriarch of the Angasan Clan moved back to the Brooks River each year to spend her summers with her family to harvest and dry the spawned out salmon on fish racks and pick berries for the winter. She would move her family to the Katmai area each spring and return to New Savonoski in the late fall. Her life was disrupted when a concession camp appeared across from her fish camp in the 1950's. The concession camp destroyed the structures located on the north side of the Brooks River to make way for the construction of the cabins for the tourists who traveled there to see the bears and catch world class rainbow on the Brooks River.

Katmai was set aside as a monument by President Woodrow Wilson on September 24, 1918. The initial boundaries were expanded in 1934 by President Herbert Hoover to protect the features of historic and scientific interests and for the protection of the brown bears, moose and other wild animals.

"Now my people don't do many of these things anymore. This is because the white man has come. He has built his highways and buildings. He says we don't have any rights. I don't know what he is talking about. We have always owned our land. Furthermore, we are citizens and we have our rights. If we are citizens, why don't we own our land? We made our claim in 1963 because the State came in and selected our land – everything, even our village and graveyard. This is not fair. We own our land – the white man does not."

— *Tanacross Chief Andrew Isaac, 1969*

As more and more tourists visited the area, Pelagia Melgonak and her family were told not to pitch their tents on the shores of the Brooks River because they were "eyesores" to the tourists. (Pelagia was my dad's aunt. She was the family matriarch. I was born in her house in Savonoski. She would raise the younger children until they were ready for school. The school was located in South Naknek. When I moved to my parents' house in South Naknek to go to school, my dad would take me and my older brother and sister who were also born at her house to spend the weekends with her.)

They would continue to harvest fish but would only return to fish after the concession camp was closed for the season. By now, they were limited in their gathering to only red fish. Red fish are spawned out sockeye salmon that is in the final stages of its life cycle. My ancestors have harvested these red fish for the past 5,000 years as documented by the archeologists who have studied the ancient village located under the site of the concession. The red fish had special spiritual value to the descendants. It connected us to our ancestors. Since the descendants could not resettle at the place of our forefathers, they returned under the dark of night to continue their sacred practice of harvesting, sensing that their ancestors were pleased with their continued practice of harvesting the red fish at the Brooks River. They felt that as long as they are able to continue this practice, they are not an abandoned people.

During the 1970's the National Park Service allowed residents of Naknek and South Naknek to fish with gillnets in Katmai National Monument. ANILCA prohibited subsistence fishing in the newly established Katmai National Park, although it does permit fishing under sport regulations. In the fall of 1981, the National Park Service formally prohibited local residents from taking red fish in the park.

At the request of the descendants of the Katmai Communities, the Bristol Bay Native Corporation drafted legislation on June 8, 1996, that would allow the Native people from the villages of Naknek, South Naknek and King Salmon to continue their harvest of red fish at the Brooks River.

Although salmon migrate to all of the streams in the Naknek Lake watershed, the Brooks River sockeye held special significance. That is where salmon have been traditionally harvested by the ancestors of the Katmai Descendants.

H.R. 4943 called the Katmai Red Fish Bill was introduced as a Public Bill onto the floor of the House of Representatives by Congressman Don Young on August 11, 1994. The bill stated: "Local residents who are descendants of Katmai residents who lived within the boundaries of the area now designated as Katmai National Park shall be permitted, subject to reasonable regulations established by the Secretary of Interior, to continue their traditional fishery for red fish in the Naknek Lake and Brooks River within the Katmai National Park." The bill was unprecedented because it would allow the harvest of salmon on the Brooks River in the Monument, which in the words of the extreme environmental community was tantamount to shooting ducks on the steps of the Lincoln Memorial.

The bill initially faced a tremendous uphill struggle with the nation's leading environmental lobby. The passage of the bill was contingent upon gaining support for the bill from the Sierra Club, the Wildlife Alliance, the Parks and Conservation Society, the State of Alaska, and the Secretary of the Department of Interior. BBNC sponsored a series of meetings with representatives of the groups and pressed for their support. The initial response was not positive. The major concern by the environmental groups was that opening up the Brooks River would compete and interfere with the world class sport fishing on the river. BBNC's response to that concern was that the red fish fishery would only be open after October 15 when the sport fish season was closed.

Another concern was that allowing a red fish fishery would impact the resource. The BBNC response was the fish that were to be harvested had already served its purpose of spawning and the fish were in the final stages of their life cycle. Another concern was that the extraction of the nearly decomposed fish would affect the nutritional needs of the rearing fish population. The BBNC response was that the harvest would be capped at

1,500 so that it would not materially affect the ecosystem. Another concern was that the fishery could cause degradation of the habitat. The response was that only boats and gill nets would be used and the nets would not be anchored. It, in effect, would be a drift fishery.

Another hurdle was the concern that the red fish fishery would create a new class of users who would come and harvest the fish for their subsistence needs. The response was that the participants would be limited to the descendants of the village of Savonoski. And finally the biggest hurdle was that it would create a subsistence fishery in a monument. The response was that if the residents wanted salmon, all they needed to do was to set their nets in front of their villages and would harvest all of their subsistence needs from the ocean fresh salmon that were swimming by in saltwater. They would not need to endure the hardship of coming to the Brooks to get their subsistence needs met. The Native way of harvesting was to harvest their needs in close proximity to the resource, as evidenced by the number of fish camps along the rivers outside the Park. The compelling point made by the BBNC was that the harvest was not for subsistence. It was a spiritual event that allowed the descendants to remember their ancestors and to connect them though the ritual of harvesting the decomposed fish. As a result of the work with the groups, there was unanimous support for the efforts of BBNC to get the red fish bill passed. It was passed on July 18, 1996, and signed into law by President Clinton in September of that year.

The Native People of Alaska must have their subsistence lifestyle protected permanently. It is the nucleus of our cultures. The solution for achieving protections for the subsistence practices of the Native People cannot be achieved by any action taken by the State of Alaska and its onerous legislature. The Alaska Constitution does not permit a separate class of harvesters. The protections for subsistence are not secure in Title VIII of ANILCA. The primary reason is that it requires that rural residents and Alaska Natives who reside in rural Alaska have the right to a subsistence priority in times of shortage. What happens when the communities in rural

Alaska lose their rural classification due to population increases? This will ultimately be the demise of the subsistence way of life of the Alaska Natives. Additionally, the federal law that authorizes the subsistence priority is always under assault by the anti-subsistence lobby. The law can be amended if they garner enough votes in the Congress to support their agenda. There is a final solution to the subsistence dilemma of the Alaska Native People.

The Alaska Federation of Natives and the Alaska Intertribal Council have joined with other statewide Native groups to develop a unified strategy on proposed legislation that would address the lack of protections for Native subsistence users. They have enlisted the support of the national Indian, faith and minority groups to lobby in support of a Native preference on subsistence. AFN representatives have traveled and met with the worldwide indigenous community. They have testified at world conferences on human rights, taking the position that subsistence for Native People is a human right.

On the congressional front, AFN and the coalition are soliciting support for a permanent solution to the subsistence protections for Alaska Natives from the friends of the American Indians in the Congress. They have developed testimony that states that Native cultural and religious ideologies can sometimes be protected under the freedom of religion policies and laws. For example, in the Carlos Frank case, the Athabascans won a lawsuit against the State of Alaska in which they had been charged for hunting a moose out of season. In this case, the moose was required for a traditional ceremony. Alaska Natives are required to feed the spirits of their ancestors.

Four federal statutes preempt Alaska state law and include specific subsistence provisions: the reindeer Industry Act of 1937, the Marine Mammal Protection Act of 1972, the Endangered Species Act of 1974 and the Alaska National Interest Lands Conservation Act of 1980. The emergence of a judicially recognized federal trust responsibility to protect Alaska Native subsistence culture and economy opens the doors for the Alaska Tribes to pursue co-management of fish and game on federal lands

"The white man came in and he took over land in secret. Nobody told us."

— *Simon Paneak, 1968*

as one way to preserve the Native way of life. As for the judicial front, the courts have concluded that the long and continuous history of federal protection constitutes statutory acceptance of a trust responsibility for the maintenance of Native subsistence culture.

8. Where are they now?

The Alaska Native Claims Settlement Act was the first real settlement between Native Americans and the federal government in which Natives were allowed to exercise self-determination. Previous treaties and settlements involved land and assets held in trust for Native people by the federal government and controlled by the Bureau of Indian Affairs.

The 44 million acres of land retained by Alaska Natives and nearly $1 billion granted to Native people are controlled by Native boards of directions of Natives corporations, and they have complete control over their assets. Although Alaska Natives had filed claims to virtually the entire state, through ANCSA, Native people retained about 12 percent of the land in the state. By contrast, the State of Alaska was granted 104 million acres of land in the Statehood Act, and the federal government controls more than 230 million acres of land, which means that together the state and federal governments control more than 85 percent of Alaska.

Some Native corporations are still waiting for completion of the land conveyance. Doyon, Ltd., which retained the most land under ANCSA, is still waiting for final conveyance of more than two million acres of its 12.5-million-acre land entitlement, according to Orie Williams, Doyon President/CEO. Williams has noted that the Association of ANCSA Regional Corporation Presidents/CEOs is working with federal government and congressional leaders to ensure that final conveyance would be completed by all Native corporations by 2009.

"This would establish the final boundaries of the state's largest private landowners – the Alaska Native Corporations – and the State of Alaska, resolving 40-year-old ownership issues," he said.

Alaska Native Corporations have made great strides and overall, they have been successful, especially when viewed in the aggregate over the

Phillip Guy discusses the formation of Calista Corp. at the first annual meeting in 1974.

Calista Corp. photo

long-term. Much remains to be done, however, to address the needs of Alaska Native people, and business corporations by their very nature are not the vehicle to solve all problems. A landmark study of Alaska Native issues was undertaken by the federal-state Alaska Natives Commission in the early 1990s, and the three-volume report released in May 1994 after nearly two years of study included many stark statistics. A sampling:

- Although more than $1.3 billion has been spent building water and sewer systems in rural Alaska, many villages have only rudimentary water and sewer utilities.
- The steep, steady rise in the Native suicide rate during the 1980s continues an upward trend that dates back to the mid-1950s; in the quarter century between 1964 and 1989, the rate of Alaska Native suicides increased 500 percent.
- The rate at which alcohol is an underlying or a contributing cause of injury death among Alaska Native is nearly triple that among non-Natives.
- Despite a nearly 80 percent increase in their per capita income between 1980 and 1990, Alaska Natives continued to be the ethnic group in Alaska with the lowest per capita income. Alaska Natives also continued to constitute the largest group of the total Alaska population to live in poverty.

The Alaska Native Policy Center of the First Alaskans Institute published a major analysis of the status of Alaska Natives in 2004, entitled, "Our Choices, Our Future." The study, prepared for the Alaska Federation of Natives, notes that Alaska has the highest percentage of Natives of any state in the nation, with a total Native population of 119,241, which is 19 percent of the state's total population of 626,932. The study shows there are still stark differences between Alaska Natives and their counterparts in Alaska and in the United States. For example, Alaska Natives commit suicide at three to four times the rate among White Americans throughout the country, and from 1999 to 2001, suicide was the fifth leading cause of death in the Alaska Native community.

The Policy Center's report notes that Native people are seeking to maintain their own cultures in a modern world of different values. The Policy Center identified four complex challenges that face Alaska Natives:

- The need for economic development and job creation and placement, which will provide family cash income, in combination with subsistence harvesting, in order to strengthen the "mixed" economic base of Native communities.
- The need to lower the cash cost-of-living for basic necessities in rural villages (e.g. electricity, fuel oil and food), in order that people can afford to live where they want to live.
- The need for healthy communities, whether in villages or urban areas, with emphasis on behavioral health, individual wellness and disease prevention.
- The need to make public schools effective community institutions that teach Native, as well as non-Native, students the basic academic skills from a culturally relevant context that is needed in a knowledge-based society.

Alaska Native Corporations cannot solve these key issues, nor were they created to do so. They likely can go a long way, though, finding creative answers.

9. A look at each of the Native regions

Ahtna, Incorporated

Total area within the region: 10 million acres
Original number of shareholders: 1,092 shareholders
Number of shareholders today: 1,150 shareholders
Total population of the region: 7,087 people

Mission Statement:

Ahtna, Incorporated, as a growth-oriented company, will enhance the overall well-being of its shareholders with monetary dividends, employment, and educational opportunities through diversified investments while continuing to encourage a strong sense of cultural pride and identity. Ahtna will implement ANCSA for the benefit of its shareholders through wise stewardship of the land and natural resources and through sustained growth for future generations.

Ahtna Region

The Ahtna Region is located in Southcentral Alaska and encompasses the Copper River Basin and the Wrangell Mountains. It is bordered to the northeast by the Mentasta and Nutzotin Mountains, to the north by the Alaska Range, to the west by the Talkeetna Mountains and to the south by the Chugach Mountains. The Wrangell Mountains are made up of dormant volcanoes with one exception. Mt. Wrangell is the largest active volcano in North America. The Ahtna Region encompasses the entire Copper

River watershed, including the Chitina, the Chistochina, the Gulkana, and the Tazlina rivers and portions of the Susitina and Tanana watersheds. The Copper River system is the fourth largest in Alaska and is the most extensively glacier-influenced. The region includes about 24,000 square miles of land, or the size of West Virginia.

People:

The Ahtna population in the Copper Basin was small and scattered because game was never plentiful enough to support large groups. Ahtna Natives traveled the river corridors, foothills, and passes of what we currently refer to as the Wrangell Mountains for several hundred years prior to European arrival in the area. They lived in semi-permanent camps, leaving for weeks at a time to hunt and to gather berries, birch wood, and other resources. Trade routes with other Native peoples were well established. Copper, found near the present-day town of McCarthy, was used for tools and for trade with other Native groups. Most villages contained 20 to 30 members of a familial clan and were situated where a major tributary entered the Copper River. There were two larger villages: Taghaelden (Taral) near the mouth of the Chitina River, and Nataelde (Batzulnetas) on Tanada Creek along the route leading northward to the Tanana and Yukon Rivers.

What they said:

"I would like to say that I think the people of Alaska are the greatest resources for the State and when we ask for 40 million – for 40 million acres – we are asking quite a bit less than what the State is getting, and I think the state should recognize and also you Senators should recognize that we Native people are the best resources of this State. And I don't see why we have to be up here fighting for our land. I don't see why someone like Peter John should have to be before me, or either a young man who is highly educated like Representative Hensley after me. I don't see why I have to be up here saying, give us back our land, when in fact the land is

Wrangell Mountains in the Ahtna Region.
Ahtna, Inc., photo

Ahtna Elders, from left, are Maggie Joe, Harry Johns, Etta Bell and Ruth Johns.

Ahtna, Inc., photo

ours. I don't see why I have to say that Cantwell is an Indian village when the whole State is a Native village. . .

Ruby Tansy, Cantwell Village,
Testimony, February 8-10, 1968.

"We get money out of this, we are going to use it for education and for building things for our children to use."

Chief Joe Goodlataw, Copper River Tribe,
testimony, February 8 - 10, 1968.

The Aleut Corporation

Total area within the region: 703,997 acres

(On March 17, 2004, The Aleut Corporation consummated a land exchange pursuant to the provisions of Section 1302(h) of ANILCA. Under this exchange TAC acquired the former Naval air facility at Adak in exchange for relinquishing over-selections it had made in the Shumagin Islands.)

Original number of shareholders: 3,249 shareholders

Number of shareholders today: 3,351 shareholders

Total population of region: about 8,000 people

Mission Statement:

Our purpose is to maximize dividends to and choices for our shareholders.

Goals

Create a healthy corporation

Generate revenues with substantial profits

Provide significant dividends and benefits to shareholders

Create meaningful linkage to the Aleut "Unangan" people

Aleut Region:

Alaska's Aleut people occupy some of the most rugged and isolated regions of the state, stretching the length of the Aleutian Chain and including the Pribilof Islands in the Bering Sea. The total land area is about the size of Rhode Island. It is from this limited land base that The Aleut Corporation, one of the 13 regional corporations established in 1971 under the terms of the Alaska Native Claims Settlement Act (ANCSA), looks to the future for its shareholders as it recognizes the history of its people.

That history reaches back some 8,000 years on the Aleutian Islands and at least 200 years in the Pribilofs. The pre-Russian population was thought to have numbered 12,000 to 15,000 people whose lives were sus-

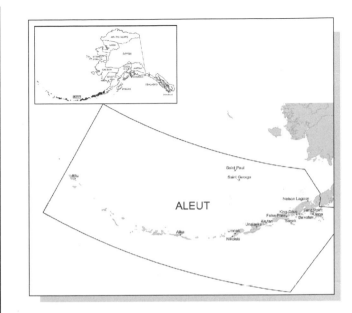

The Holy Ascension Russian Orthodox Church in Unalaska.
The Aleut Corp. photo

tained by the sea.

The early Russian period, some 250 years ago, brought profound change to the Aleut people. Russian fur traders enslaved entire villages; their inhabitants were pressed into service hunting sea mammals for fur and then relocated to serve the Russian's colonization goals.

With the purchase of Alaska by the United States in 1867, the Russian dominance ended, but the Russian influence on Aleut culture remains to this day. The Russian Orthodox faith continues to be a strong element of Aleut cultural heritage.

Today, that enduring heritage is blended with 20th-century business endeavors by The Aleut Corporation. Launched with an ANCSA settlement of $19.5 million, 66,000 acres surface land and 1.5 million acres of subsurface estate, the corporation issued stock to 3,249 shareholders. Today, The Aleut Corporation pays dividends to over 3,500 shareholders.

The corporation's early economic activities centered on the commercial fishing industry. With new fisheries about to open and the expansion of processing facilities on Adak, it's clear The Aleut Corporation's strong ties to the sea are not about to be compromised. That said, investment in real estate, primarily in Southcentral Alaska, along with rock and gravel extraction from corporate land are also key parts of the corporation's portfolio. The Aleut Corporation also participates in the Small Business Administration's 8(a) program. The certification provides competitive advantages to minority-owned companies that pursue federal contracts. The Aleut Corporation subsidiaries have flourished as a result of their 8(a) status.

The greatest opportunities and challenges for the corporation are yet to come. In the spring of 2004 Adak Island, the one-time Naval Air Facility that housed 6,000 military and support personnel was officially conveyed to The Aleut Corporation from the U.S. Navy, U.S. Dept. of Interior and the State of Alaska. Adak is rich in potential and is already proving an excellent investment.

In 2004 The Aleut Corporation announced the highest shareholder dividend ever. It is with great determination and a strong sense of cultural identity that The Aleut Corporation faces its future in Alaska.

People:

The Aleutian Islands' cultural history dates back at least 8,000 years. The region has been inhabited by the "Unangas" (Aleut people). Rough, windy seas surround the volcanic islands. Inhabitants experience some of the most inclement weather in the world. The Unangas are excellent navigators of the sea and designed sea vessels called "baidarkas." Men were outfitted with "kamleikas" (waterproof garments). Women were expert and artful grass weavers, who made baskets, sleep mats, wall dividers, hand mittens, and foot coverings. Some baskets were woven so tightly they could contain water. Grass was woven so tightly that mittens and grass foot coverings repelled water. Unangas' homes were called "barabaras" which were semi-subterranean homes covered by earth and grass with entries through the roof.

What they said:

"One of the serious problems on the Native education is the separation that has been demanded between the child, the family and the community. If this practice is permitted to continue we will negate the whole educational progress. We must adhere to the concept of the community school.

". . .The community must feel that it too is educating the child and to accept this transmission there must be both bilingualism and cultural pluralism."

Flore Lekanof,
written testimony, July 12, 1968.

"The Cannikin detonation threatens possible destruction or most serious harm to the lives, property, commerce and culture of the Native people living in the Aleutian Island area."

Iliodor Philemonof,
President, Aleut League

Atka Aleut Dancers.

The Aleut Corp. photo

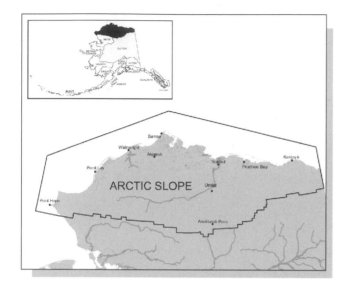

Arctic Slope Regional Corporation

Total area within the region: 57 million acres
Original number of shareholders: 3,738 shareholders
Number of shareholders today: 10,000 shareholders*
Total population of the region: 7,385 people

* Because ASRC shareholders voted to add on children born after 1971, the corporation estimates that 30 shareholders are added to the corporate rolls each month

Mission Statement

To actively manage our lands, resources, diversified operating subsidiaries and investments throughout the world in order to enhance Inupiat cultural and economic freedoms.

Arctic Slope Region

The Arctic Slope Region encompasses 89,000 square miles or an area about the size of the state of Minnesota. There are eight communities in the region with villages ranging from populations as small as 200 and up to 5,000 people.

The environment is limited to shrubby or mat-like vegetation called alpine tundra which encircles the North Pole and extends to the taiga to the south. Alpine tundra is found high on mountains above the altitudes that trees can grow. The climate is Arctic. Temperatures range from -56 degrees below zero during the winter months to an average of 45 degrees during the summer months. In Barrow, the northernmost community in Alaska, the sun remains hidden below the horizon for three months each year. Precipitation is light, at 5 inches, with snowfall averaging 20 inches.

People:

The word "Inupiat" means "the real people." The Inupiat have inhabited the Arctic since time immemorial, traditionally following animal migrations and subsisting on whale, caribou, walrus, seal, fish and water fowl. In one of the earth's most challenging environments, the Inupiat developed a rich culture and a dynamic set of traditions. Their survival depended on close family ties, a strong sense of community and a deep respect for nature. Today, the Inupiat still look to the land for cultural and economic sustenance. Despite changes in technology and lifestyle, most Inupiat still depend on hunting and fishing for cultural identity and partial income.

Whaling is the hallmark of Inupiat society. When a whaling captain lands a bowhead whale, it provides an opportunity for the entire community to come together for sharing and celebration. During Nalukataq, the summer festival celebrating a successful whale harvest, hundreds of people gather to share in the feast and enjoy Eskimo dancing.

What they said:

"There was no war, we maintain that we were never conquered."

Joe Upicksoun,
October 16, 1996, Anchorage Daily News

"First of all, this is our land, and we wish that your society had never come and, now that you are here, that you would leave, that you would get out."

Eben Hopson, Executive Director,
Arctic Slope Native Association, Written testimony.

"I never really did understand what being a landlord was all about until I started reading books about the Lower 48 Indians, how they were treat-

Nicole Harcharek and son Ashtyn on the tundra outside of Barrow.
Photo courtesy of Chris Arend

Whalebones outside of Barrow.

Photo courtesy of Chris Arend

ed. . .And I was determined then that this thing that happened in the Lower 48 states would never happen to our people up here."

Joe Upicksoun

"This is a land claims effort; it is not a social welfare bill; it is our ability as Arctic Slope. . .to own the land. Owning land, we can develop it and get economic benefits if those lands we selected were rich in terms of minerals. . .surface and subsurface."

Joe Upicksoun

Bering Straits Native Corporation

Total area within the region: 14.7 million acres
Original number of shareholders: 6,330 shareholders
Number of shareholders today: 6,334 shareholders
Total population of the region: 9,196 people

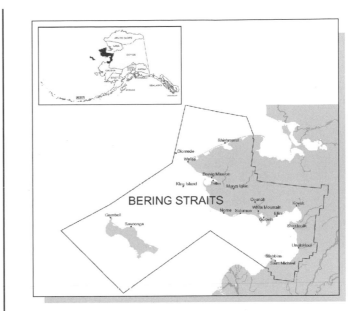

Mission statement:

To improve the quality of life of our people through economic development while protecting our culture and heritage.

Bering Straits Region

The regional boundaries extend 230 miles east to west and 230 miles north to south and encompass an area of more than 26,000 square miles, roughly the size of the state of West Virginia. The land is made up mostly of Arctic tundra and taiga. There are three culturally distinct groups of Inuit people who inhabit the region. Inupiat reside on the Seward Peninsula and the King and Diomede islands. The Central Yup'ik primarily reside in the villages south of Unalakleet, and Siberian Yupik live on St. Lawrence Island. Average winter temperature is a low of 2 degrees and a high of 13 degrees. In the summer, the average low is 45 and the high is 56.

People

The Eskimo people have lived in this region as an identifiable culture for at least 3,000 years; the earliest documented evidence of human habitation dates back 10,000 to 11,000 years. Settlements concentrate along the coast and river systems, for the sea was and is the principal focus of human activities. The Eskimos call themselves Inuit or "Real People." Traditional subsistence patterns depend upon location and season of the resources, such as whales, marine mammals, fish, caribou, and plants.

King Island Singers and Dancers carry on the traditions of their island's culture.

Bering Straits Native Corp. photo

Whales and sea mammals were hunted in the coastal and island villages. Pink and chum salmon; cod, inconnu and whitefish were fished whenever ice formed; herring and crab and halibut were also caught. Also birds and eggs formed an important part of the diet.

What they said:

"We hope that after the passage of the bill we will be allowed to start helping ourselves instead of waiting for a handout or permission to do what we know is best for our own interests."

Jerome Trigg, *of the Seward Peninsula Native Association, testimony, Feb. 8 - 10, 1968.*

"When I was growing up, things were different, you weren't outspoken about being a Native. But my kids are outspoken. They're proud to tell people that they are Eskimo and that they eat Eskimo food. The word up here is Eskimo."

Carol Drake, *Alaska Native Land Claims*

Inupiaq in the Bering Straits Region have been driving caribou into enclosed areas as a hunting technique for thousands of years; this site above has been used for this technique for more than 200 years.

Bering Straits Native Corp. photo

Bristol Bay Native Corporation

Total area within the region: 34 million acres
Original number of shareholders: 5,401 shareholders
Number of shareholders today: 7,456 shareholders
Total population of the region: 8,003 people

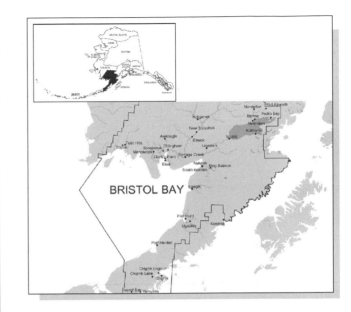

Mission Statement
Enriching our Native way of life

Bristol Bay Region

At 34 million acres, the Bristol Bay region is slightly larger than the State of Ohio. The region has spectacular landscapes, a fascinating and complex history, three diverse Native cultural traditions, volcanoes, unspoiled wilderness, and diverse state and national parks and refuges. In addition to 8,000 residents, Bristol Bay is home to abundant wildlife – 10,000 brown bears, 25,000 walrus, and 25 million salmon, plus fresh water seals, ospreys, eagles, and many other species. Among the wide-open spaces are black sand beaches, mountain ranges, lowland tundra, wetlands, abundant flora and fauna, and many wild and scenic rivers. Lake Iliamna, located in the north of the region, is the largest freshwater lake in Alaska.

The Bristol Bay villages are situated in the watershed of the world-renowned Bristol Bay salmon fishery. The pristine lakes and rivers that empty into Bristol Bay support spawning and harvesting of all five species of Pacific salmon – king, sockeye, silver, chum, and pink – as well as rainbow trout, arctic char, grayling, northern pike, lake trout and Dolly Varden. Beluga whales and Orcas (killer whales) can be seen following the salmon runs. The area is home to caribou, moose, bear, and walrus, as well as small game such as beaver, porcupine, otter, and fox, and varied waterfowl.

The Peter Pan Seafoods Cannery in Dillingham.

BBNC photo

All wildlife is important for the subsistence lifestyle and for the commercial and sport activities of local communities. Wood-Tikchik State Park (the largest state park system in the United States), Togiak National Wildlife Refuge, and Round Island State Game Sanctuary are all accessible from Dillingham and Naknek.

People

Traditional customs of the Eskimo, Aleut, and Athabascan are still evident. Each of the three Native peoples of the Bristol Bay region has their own distinct Native language and dialect that identifies them as being different from another tribe. Local arts and crafts can be seen in the region's museums and visitor centers. From hub communities, visitors can enjoy wildlife viewing, boating, rafting, fishing, hunting, traditional subsistence activities, air tours, hiking, cannery tours, museum tours, and historic sites.

What they said:

"The monetary settlement will help the Native to help himself to become equipped with the skills and the education needed to effectively compete in our modern society and to improve the health and living conditions from which he now suffers. But this process of transition from the Native way of life to the modern white man's way of life will take time and we need the land to sustain us during that period as well as contribute to our economic base."

Herman Schroeder and Harvey Samuelsen,
Bristol Bay Native Association, 1969

"Land is the gift of our ancestors and the guarantee of our right to continue our subsistence lifestyle. Land is the heart of our culture. Without the land, we are nothing.

Harvey Samuelsen,
Bristol Bay Village Leadership Workshop, 2001

Calista Corporation

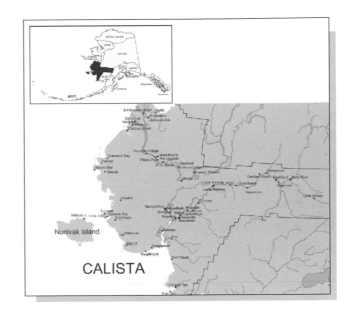

Total area within the region: 35.84 million acres
Original number of shareholders: 13,306 shareholders
Current number of shareholders: 12,483 shareholders
Total population for the region: 23,034 people

Mission Statement
To continue growth and profits through teamwork, professionalism, and innovation while respecting cultural values.

People
Three Alaska Native culture groups are found in the southwest portion of the state, Yup'ik, Cup'ik, and Athabascan. The traditional Native culture of this area remains largely intact, in part due to the fact that Russian explorers did not venture into the region until the 1800s. The Yup'ik language is still prevalent within the region (approximately 70 percent of people in the region speak Yup'ik) and traditional focus on the extended family as the center of social life remains a foundation of the community.

Historically, the people of this region were mobile – following the migration of animals and fish, or the availability of edible greens and berries. (The southwest region is rich in birds and mammals, particularly large game such as bear, moose, and caribou. Communities near the sea subsist on whales, seal, walrus and an abundant supply of fish.) Seasonal camps were established along meandering waterways where food was most plentiful. Many of today's villages have grown from these ancient seasonal camps and the numerous waterways function as roads across the flat, marshy planes which characterize the region.

The late Elder David Jackson of Kwethluk is shown with two children.

Calista Corp. photo

What they said:

"The land is the provider. We cannot own the land, because the land owns us. I can go anywhere, and if I have a gun, I can survive. A gun and a shaker of salt, that's all I need."

William Tyson of Anchorage and St. Mary's (1985)

"If a person has none of the teachings, he will be like someone lost in a blizzard. But the person who has teachings will derive strength from them and use them like a walking stick to prevent himself from getting hurt."

Marie Nichols of Kasigluk, shareholder,
Anchorage Daily News, Jan. 31, 1989

"We must prevail, not fail, for the good of our society. And so let us be united in all what we do and try to achieve our dreams united, not divided, for our own sake and our children and their children's sake."

James Charlie of Toksook Bay,
shareholder, Tundra Times, March 13, 1989

Children assist at a fish camp at Toksook Bay.

Calista Corp. photo

Chugach Alaska Corporation

Total area within the region: 9.6 million acres
Original number of shareholders: 1,991 shareholders
Number of shareholders today: 2,097 shareholders
Total population of the region: 11,791 people

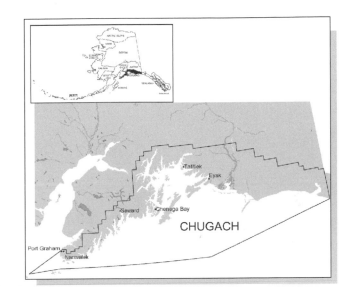

Mission Statement
Committed to profitability, celebration of heritage and ownership of our land.

Chugach Region
The Chugach Region comprises 15,625 square miles in Southcentral Alaska or about the size of Massachusetts and New Jersey combined. The Chugach Region extends on the west from the southern tip of the Kenai Peninsula eastward to the 141st meridian near the Malaspina Glacier between Icy Bay and Yakutat. The regional boundary rarely extends more than 50 miles inland, roughly following a line which approximates the crest of the Kenai and the Chugach Mountain ranges. A large portion of the region is overlain by three of the major icefields of North America, the Harding, Sargent and Bagley Icefields, each spawning numerous glaciers which still reach to the sea. At its geographic center is Prince William Sound.

People
Chugach Alaska Corporation (CAC) is comprised of three Alaska Native cultures: The Chugach people, who are of Aleut/Eskimo descent, are the prominent Native culture in the region. Three other Indian cultures in the region are the Eyak, Athabascan and Tlingit Indians who have occupied the eastern portion of the region. The Chugach people primarily

Jamie Johnson, wearing traditional Alutiiq clothing, participates in the Nuuqciq Spirit Camp on Nuchek Island in Prince William Sound.

Chugach Alaska Corp. photo

inhabited the coastal area in Prince William Sound (lower Cook Inlet). In part because of the coastal accessibility to the people, their rich history includes a strong Russian influence.

The Chugach are the dominant Native group in the Sound. The name Chugach (pronounced "CHOO-gatch") covers most of the coastal Native groups. Other names denote sub-tribes (with the exception of the Eyak). The Eyak (pronounced "EE-yak") are of Indian descent. Within the Chugach Alaska Natives, there are sub-tribes, all of whom share a common ancestry, but who were isolated in different parts of the Sound. The lands and waters are rich in timber, minerals, and wildlife resources. The Sound's majestic fiords, bays, and waterways are home to a diverse population of fish, marine mammals, and birds. The land's diversity ranges from glacier and mountains to dense forests of hemlock and spruce that thrive here.

What they said:

"Across the Unites States, and other places, Alaska Native Corporations are contributing to the efficiency and modernization of the United States government which is so necessary in this time of global challenge and threats."

Sheri Buretta, Chugach Chairman,
CEOs letter spring 2005.

"We have lots of tools and institutions at our disposal, but I'm also reminded that it doesn't really matter what institutions you have or what laws you have if the people themselves don't have the will to survive and go forward. That is what I have sensed more than anything in the Native community over the last 20 to 30 years — the will to accomplish things for the next generation, the desire to pull together and work together no matter if you're from the Slope or you're from Southeast.

Julie Kitka, Commemorating 30 Years of ANCSA
at the Alaska Native Heritage Center

"Very few of the Native people were employed to work for the cannery. The foreigners in the cannery used fish traps to take most of the fish from the area. Hundreds of thousands of fish were taken from time to time by means of the fishtraps and eventually most of the fishing for the Native people was destroyed. After the fishtraps were used it was very hard for my people to make a living. Nobody ever paid any attention to us. They did not want to give us jobs, nor were we able to make a good living by hunting, fishing, and trapping.

Walter Meganack, of Port Graham, testimony, Feb. 8 - 10, 1968.

Nuchek Island is an 800-acre island located in one of the bays of Hinchenbrook Island in Prince William Sound.
Chugach Alaska Corp. photo

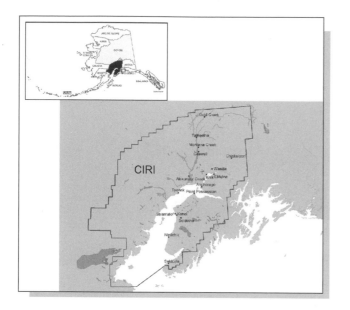

CIRI

Total area within the region: 24 million acres
Original number of shareholders: 6,243 shareholders
Number of shareholders today: 7,000 shareholders
Total population of the region: 260,263 people

Mission Statement

The mission of CIRI is to promote the economic and social well-being and Alaska Native heritage of our shareholders, now and into the future, through prudent stewardship of the company's resources, while furthering self-sufficiency among CIRI shareholders and their families.

The Cook Inlet Region

The Cook Inlet Region, located in Southcentral Alaska, is 38,000 square miles, or almost the size of Virginia. The region is home to several mountain ranges and glaciers; its vegetation includes lowland black spruce forests. Bottomland spruce-poplar forests are adjacent to larger river drainages, along with thickets of alder and willow. Some wet tundra communities exist along the Cook Inlet coastline. Major river systems in the area include the Susitna River, Kenai River, and Matanuska River. The Cook Inlet area, known by Dena'ina people today as either Tikahtnu or Nuti, stretches from Seldovia near the southern end of the Kenai Peninsula to just south of the Talkeetna Mountains and the towering mountains of Denali National Park and Preserve. The western boundaries are the Alaska Range, including the Lake Clark National Park and Preserve, meandering south to the Katmai National Park and Preserve. The eastern boundaries of the irregularly shaped region are the eastern and northern portions of the Harding Ice Fields near Seward and the Kenai Fjords National Park, moving north to the Kenai-Chugach Mountains.

People

While other Alaska Native Corporations are primarily representative of their Native villages, CIRI is the corporation of Alaska's urban center, Anchorage, where many Alaska Natives relocated from other regions. Thus, CIRI has a unique cultural diversity. CIRI shareholders represent a cross-section of all Alaska Native cultures, including Athabascan, Tlingit, Haida, and Tsimshian Indians, Yup'ik, Cup'ik, Alutiiq, and Inupiat Eskimos, and Aleuts. Approximately one-third of its shareholders reside in Anchorage, one-third in other areas of Alaska, and one-third in other states across the continental U.S. However, Dena'ina Athabascans primarily inhabit the villages within the region (Eklutna, Tyonek, Knik, Kenai, Salamantof, and Point Possession). The people of the village of Chickaloon are a mixture of Ahtna and Dena'ina Athabascan, and the people of the villages of Ninilchik and Seldovia have ancestors of Aleut and Alutiiq descent, as well as some Dena'ina. The Dena'ina are the only Athabascan group who lived near saltwater. Consequently, they utilized the marine resources of the region and adapted much of the marine technology of their neighbors and, in former times, sworn enemies, the Chugach Alutiiq.

Emil McCord has been a leader in the village of Tyonek for many years.
Tundra Times photo

What they said:

"I urge you and your committee to study this situation carefully and see what can be done for the Natives to determine their own destiny, so that we can live our own life as first-class citizens of the United States of America."

George Ondola, *Chairman, Village Council of Eklutna, testimony, Feb. 8 - 10, 1968.*

Ravynn Nothstine has learned much about her Inupiaq culture through dancing with an Anchorage dance group.
CIRI photo

Originally named Renard Island, Fox Island is located in Resurrection Bay and is a tourist attraction for CIRI Alaska Tourism Corp.

CIRI photo

"Visitors look around and say, 'There are no Native people here.' Well, we've been right here for 200 years, but nobody ever paid attention."

Clare Swan,
Anchorage Daily News, December 15, 1991

"Dena'ina galeq qbegh qighestle k'usht'a k'el qihtilnesh, qudiq' q'u k'ech' qulyu.   . . .The Dena'ina didn't have any books, and they didn't read, but they had beliefs of their own."

Peter Kalifornsky, *A Dena'ina Legacy, Page 73.*

Doyon, Limited

Total area within the region: 131 million acres
Original number of shareholders: 9,061 shareholders
Number of shareholders today: 14,000 shareholders
Total population of the region: 95,565 people

Mission Statement

To continually enhance our position as a financially strong Native corporation in order to promote the economic and social well-being of our shareholders and future shareholders, to strengthen our native way of life and to protect and enhance our land and resources.

Doyon Region

The size of Alaska's Interior is 190,477 square miles or the about the size of Colorado and Utah combined. The vegetation ranges from the boreal forest to above the Arctic Circle with rolling taiga and tundra. It is a land of extremes. In the summer it can reach into the high 80's and in the winter it can dip to -50 below. However the average high in the winter is -2 below and in the low is about -20. In the summer the average high is 70 and the low is 50. The Interior is home to the largest mountain in North America, Mt. McKinley. The people of the Doyon Region called it Deenaalee or Denali, its official name in the state, which means the high or tall one. With the land entitlement of 12.5 million acres, Doyon is the largest private landowner in Alaska and is one of the largest private landowners in North America. The corporation's lands extend from the Brooks Range on the north to the Alaska Range on the south. The Alaska Canada border is our eastern border and the western portion almost reaches the Norton Sound.

Mt. Fairplay, about 30 miles northeast of Tok, dominates the landscape in this Interior Alaska photo.

Doyon photo

People

Doyon shareholders are of Athabascan descent. Athabascan people lived a semi-nomadic existence, moving from camp to camp. They lived in small groups, often composed of extended family and led by the most skillful and accomplished hunter. Temporary shelters were made with branches and moose hides. Permanent structures were made of bark, moss or sod. Athabascans relied on moose, caribou, fowl, fish, beaver, muskrats, porcupine, and other animals. Birch bark and spruce roots were used to make containers to cook in or store berries. Canoes were made with huge pieces of birch bark bound together with young spruce roots and sealed with spruce sap. Willow and spruce were used to make fishtraps, snowshoes, and bows and arrows. Tanned moose hide skins and fur were used for summer and winter clothing. Athabascan women are well known for creating magnificent beaded baby belts, moose hide gun covers, and moccasins.

What they said:

"Native leaders in Alaska have given great attention to the structure of the settlement, the means of administering the land and money. Indeed the concept of the development corporations is ours, though we would divide the land and money among three levels of business corporations, local, regional and statewide, in keeping with the pluralism of American society and economy."

Alfred Ketzler, President, Tanana Chiefs Conference, Nenana

"A cultural bulldozer has swept across Alaska dragging my people with it."

Donald Peter, Fort Yukon, written testimony

"Gentlemen, the future of the State of Alaska and the future of its citizens is tremendous and beyond belief. It is like a leap from the dark ages to the atomic age. . ."

John Sackett, President of Tanana Chiefs Conference, testimony, Feb. 8 - 10, 1968.

"A man without a title under his feet, he loses something. He doesn't have authority."

Claude Demientieff, Galena, testimony, Feb. 8 - 10, 1968.

Georgiana Lincoln, who served in the Alaska Legislature for 14 years, is shown meeting with Nelson Angapak in this 1977 photo.
Nelson Angapak photo

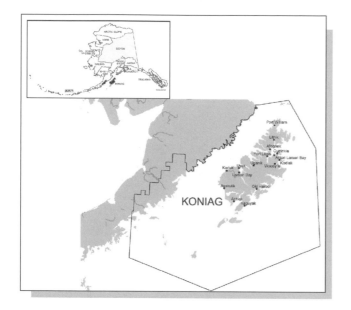

Koniag, Inc.

Total area within the region: 4.6 million acres
Original number of shareholders: 3,400 shareholders
Number of shareholders today: 3,600 shareholders
Total population of the region: 15,000 people

Mission Statement

To optimize profits to provide dividends and benefits while preserving our cultural pride.

The Koniag Region

The Kodiak Island Archipelago is a large group of islands about 30 miles off the coast of Alaska. The archipelago is about 177 miles long and encompasses nearly 5,000 square miles, roughly the size of the state of Connecticut. At 3,588 square miles, Kodiak Island is the largest island in the group and the second largest island in the United States. Only the island of Hawaii is larger. It has several peaks that are 3,000 feet to 4,000 feet tall. Also there are 40 small cirque glaciers. The climate in the summer averages 50-54 degrees and 10-25 degrees in the winter. Another interesting fact is that the region experiences an average 54 inches of precipitation throughout the year.

People

The Alutiiq are one of eight Native Alaska peoples and they have inhabited the coastal environments of Southcentral Alaska for many thousands of years. Their traditional homelands include Prince William Sound, the outer Kenai Peninsula, the Kodiak Archipelago and the Alaska Peninsula. People lived in large coastal villages and hunted sea mammals from skin-covered kayaks. The Alutiiq share many cultural practices with the other coastal peoples, particularly the Aleut of the Aleutian chain and the Yup'ik of the Bering Sea coast. Anthropologists believe these cultural similarities reflect a common ancestry. At the time of European colonization, the Alutiiq were divided into three regional groups, each speaking a slightly different dialect of the Alutiiq language. Today about 4,000 Alutiiq people live in 15 rural villages, five towns and each of Alaska's major cities. There are about 1,630 Alutiiq people in the Kodiak Archipelago. About half live in six villages – Akhiok, Karluk, Larsen Bay, Old Harbor, Ouzinkie and Port Lions. About 900 people reside in the City of Kodiak. These communities represent a small percentage of the Alutiiq villages once occupied. In the early 1800s there were more than 60 Alutiiq villages in the Kodiak Archipelago.

Alaina Lukin models traditional Alutiiq clothing.
Koniag Inc. photo

What they said:

"APA (Alaska Packers Association) didn't can anything but reds. They just threw the rest of the fish away. The canneries very seldom ever hired Natives, they usually brought their own workers."

*Larry Matfay, Kodiak Area Native Association,
Testimony, Feb. 8-10, 1968.*

"Kodiak I think won a place in the hearts of all of us…. I feel as if I wanted to go back, to Kodiak, almost as if I could return there to live. So secluded, so remote, so peaceful; such a mingling of the domestic, the pastoral, the sylvan, with the wild and the rugged; such emerald heights, such flowery vales, such blue arms and recesses of the sea, and such a vast green solitude stretching away to the west, and to the north and to the south."

*John Burroughs, Bewitching Alaska!:
The Harriman Expedition, 1899*

Old Woman's Lake on Kodiak Island.
Koniag Inc. photo

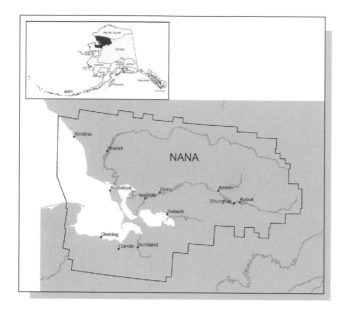

NANA Regional Corporation, Inc.

Total area within the region: 24.3 million acres
Original number of shareholders: 4,828 shareholders
Number of shareholders today: 10,295 shareholders
Total population of the region: 7,300 people

Mission statement

We improve the quality of life for our people by maximizing economic growth, protecting and enhancing our lands, and promoting healthy communities with decisions, actions, and behaviors inspired by our Inupiat Ilitqusiat values, and consistent with NANA's core principles.

Inupiat Ilitqusiat

Every Inupiaq is responsible to all other Inupiat for the survival of our cultural spirit, and the values and traditions through which it survives. Through our extended family, we retain, teach and live our Inupiaq way.

With guidance and support from Elders, we must teach our children Inupiaq values:

- Knowledge of Language
- Knowledge of Family Tree
- Sharing
- Humility
- Respect for Others
- Love for Children
- Cooperation
- Hard Work
- Respect for Elders
- Respect for Nature

- Avoid Conflict
- Family Roles
- Humor
- Spirituality
- Domestic Skills
- Hunter Success
- Responsibility to Tribe

NANA Region

The NANA Region is 36,000 square miles or about the size of Indiana. The large rivers that run through it are the Kobuk, Selawik, and Noatak. The terrain ranges from mountains, hills, sand dunes, swamps, flood plains, coastal plains, barrier beaches and spits. The climate varies between: 40 to 60 degrees in the summer and between -15 to -20 below in the winter, with an annual rainfall of 9 inches including 40 inches of snow.

People

The Inupiat have inhabited this region for over 10,000 years. The ancestral Inupiat crossed the Bering Land Bridge from Siberia during the period many thousands of years ago when sea level was much lower than it is now. The ancestral Inupiat crossed the Bering Land Bridge from Siberia. Some of the early migrants continued their journeys on to the east and south. They were skilled hunters and gatherers and subsisted on whale, fish, caribou, and moose, supplementing their diet with the berry and root plants native to this region. The hardy Inupiat people survived the challenges of adapting to the harsh Arctic climate and maintained their culture based on cooperation and sharing. The Inupiat people rely heavily on subsistence hunting and fishing. Whaling has been at the core of Inupiaq. Bowhead whales weigh one ton or more and can easily reach 60 feet in length.

Julia Mills models a traditional Inupiaq parka in Noatak.
NANA Regional Corp. photo

Boats are beached at Kivalina.

NANA Regional Corp. photo

What they said:

"The task force (AFN, State and Interior officials named in 1967-68) further believes that the use of a corporate form of organization would enable the village and regional groups to participate in modern economy."

Willie Hensley, Testimony, February 8 - 10, 1968.

"The Alaska Native seeks not to isolate himself from the State – but to become a moving and dynamic part of the State – and we feel that a resolution of the lands problems will enable us to participate in the development of the State, rather than be a burden in the progress that we see on the Alaska horizon."

Willie Hensley, Testimony, Feb. 8 - 10, 1968.

"The whole idea was to have the land protected for our use."

John Schaeffer, former NANA president

Robert Newlin was the first chairman of the NANA Regional Corp. board.

NANA Regional Corp. photo

Sealaska

Total area within the region: 17 million acres
Original number of shareholders: 15,800 shareholders
Number of shareholders today: 17,400 shareholders
Total population of the region: 70,082 people

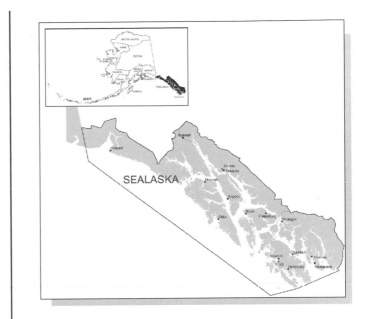

Mission Statement
- Maximize return on assets with a prudent level of risk
- Increase shareholder equity
- Maximize dividends and other shareholder benefits for the purpose of enhancing the shareholders' quality of life

Sealaska Region
Southeast Alaska is 37,943 square miles. The region is larger than the state of Indiana. It is a lush northern rain forest, with tidewater glacier fiords, massive ice fields, rugged mountains and extraordinary wildlife, on land and sea. Dense forests of western hemlock, Sitka spruce, Alaska yellow cedar and red cedar have thrived in the heavy rainfall and mild climate.

People
Southeast Alaska was owned and occupied by the Tlingit and Haida. In the historic period, Tsimshians from Canada migrated into Alaska and were granted a reservation by Congress. The Southeast Alaska Indians occupied a territory abundant in natural resources. From this they developed a complex culture and sophisticated art tradition.

The underlying basis of the Native cultures of Southeast Alaska is embodied in their core value that recognizes the importance of maintaining spiritual and social balance. Their primary social unit is the clan, and social balance between Eagle and Raven clans must be maintained to ensure the well-being of their society. They also have obligations to their

Juneau is the largest community in Southeast Alaska, and it is Alaska's State Capitol.

Todd Antioquia photo

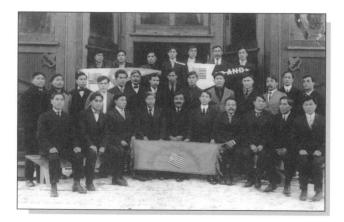

Shown at the Alaska Native Brotherhood Convention at Sitka in 1914 are: first row, from left, James Watson, Juneau; Frank Mercer, Juneau; Herbert Murchison, Metlakatla; Chester Worthington, Wrangell; Peter Simpson, Sitka; Paul Liberty, Sitka; the Rev. Edward Marsden, Metlakatla; Haines DeWitt, Kake; Mark Jacobs Sr., Sitka; Charles Newton, Kake. Second row, from left, John Willard, Sitka; Woosk-Kee-Nah (Jim Johnson); Seward Kunz, Juneau; Stephen Nickles, Sitka; Donald Austin, Wrangell; George McKay, Saxman; Cyrus Peck Sr., Sitka; Eli Katanook, Angoon; Charles Daniel, Sitka; Don Cameron, Sitka; Ralph Young, Hoonah; Rudolph Walton, Sitka; William S. Jackson, Sitka; Frank D. Price Sr., Sitka. Third row, from left, James Gordon, Klukwan; Andrew Hope, Sitka; George Bartlett, Sitka; Tommie Williams, Sitka; John Williams, Sitka; George Lewis, Sitka; Sergius Williams, Sitka.

Alaska State Library photo

ancestors and well as future generations. The Southeast Alaska Indians also believe that they have special spiritual relationships to the land and wildlife. These relationships are evidenced through the crest art owned by clans. Crest art unites clan members and depicts the relationship of individuals to the land and wildlife. Their traditional beliefs and practices are most evident in their rich ceremonial life and memorial rituals which are commonly referred to as "potlatches." Their traditional values and worldview are the basis of their cultural survival into the present-day period.

What they said:

"Your constitution promises that the property rights of all men – not just white men – shall be safeguarded. . . .We have decided that the real reason why our possessions are being taken from us is that we are human beings, and not wolves or bears. The men from Washington have set aside many millions of acres on which wolves and bears may not be disturbed, and nobody objects to that. Perhaps if we were wolves or bears we could have just as much protection. But we are only human beings. There are no closed seasons when it comes to skinning Alaska Natives."

Amy Hallingstad (Tlingit) - Letter to Mrs. Ruth Muskrat Bronson
Secretary of National Congress of American Indians (date unknown)

". . .the conviction that we had better take something, or lose everything. Or yielding to the sweet surrender of our seducer, we can clasp to our bosom the price that we are to give for surrendering to 40 million acres of land which is ours to begin with. It's a wonderful real estate transaction."

William Paul, Sr., testimony, Feb. 8 - 10, 1968.

"It is widely held among Natives that we must conform to the demands made of us in the development process. It must be said that conformity does not necessarily imply total integration. Most Natives feel that it is vital to our development to maintain a unique cultural identity, an identification with our history and cultural values. The dichotomy here is not harmful, but rather is conducive to a more realistic and full conformity."

Byron Mallott, Testimony, Feb. 8 - 10, 1968.

"The corporate provisions of S. 2906 providing for the establishment of village, regional corporations, and a statewide corporation owned and operated solely by, and for the betterment of Alaska's Natives – I submit will, if made reality, be one of the most significant development stories in Alaska's history. With this opportunity the Natives will prove conclusively their worth as productive citizens both to the State of Alaska and the Nation. Freed of their own volition and by their accomplishments, from dependency upon the Government, the Native of Alaska will be able to take his rightful place in this Nation, and the Government will be freed from this haunting responsibility in a nation of plenty."

Byron Mallott, Testimony, Feb. 8 - 10, 1968.

"This would be in accord with the highest principles of self-determination and would insure the opportunity for our people to learn through participation in the processes attendant to corporation activities."

John Borbridge, Jr., President of the Central Council of the Tlingit and Haida Indians, testimony, Feb. 8 - 10, 1968.

Angoon was destroyed by the U.S. Navy in 1882.
JoAnn George drawing

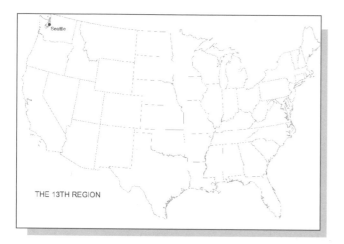

THE 13TH REGION

The 13th Regional Corporation

Original number of shareholders: 4,537 shareholders
Number of shareholders today: 6,000 shareholders

Mission Statement
Our mission is to allocate resources for our subsidiaries to flourish and oversee investments for the benefit of our shareholders.

Vision Statement
Our vision is fostering our Alaska Native heritage.

People
The 13th Regional Corporation was created last to represent those Natives who did not reside in the State of Alaska.

As provided under the 1971 Alaska Native Claims Settlement Act, and by a 1975 U.S. District Court ruling in Washington, D.C., the 13th Regional Corporation was formed under Alaska Law as a private for-profit entity on December 19, 1975. Its creation hinged on how many of the approximately 78,000 Alaska Native people eligible to be enrolled under the federal law marked Section 22 of the official enrollment form with a "yes" vote. A ruling from Judge Oliver Gasch overturned the Bureau of Indian Affairs' initial determination that an insufficient number of enrollees voted for the creation of the 13th. Prior to the ruling, the 4,537 persons who were later to become 13th Regional Corporation shareholders were all designated as shareholders in one of the other 12 regional corporations. The corporation began with 4,537 shareholders and currently has approximately 6,000 shareholders. All the other corporations share in revenue generated through sales of minerals, timber and other valuable resources from these selected lands through a revenue pooling provision of ANCSA.

What they said:

"When I became responsible for the company, it was $14 million in debt and had assets of $3 million. My strategy was to do whatever it took. My goal was to regain everything was lost by those before us."

Kurt Engelstad, former president of 13th Region, Between Worlds 1998.

"We hope to get a land base, I am very, very hopeful that we will get land like the other regional corporations in Alaska."

Norman Ream, President of 13th Region, Between Worlds 1998.

The Northern Stars dance group is a mixed group of Alaska Natives.

Thirteenth Regional Corp. photo

Thirteenth Region shareholders gather in Seattle for the 2004 Annual Shareholders Picnic.

Thirteenth Region photo

135

Chief Gary Harrison
Southcentral Foundation photo

10. Then Came the Land Claims

By Chief Gary Harrison, Chickaloon

I am Chief Gary Harrison of Chickaloon Village, a leader of the Aht'na t'ana Dena from Alaska. Before the Treaty of Cession in 1867, the Indigenous Peoples of Alaska traded with whomever came around, and they roamed and took care of the piece of Mother Earth that they were in. Their many beliefs ruled their day-to-day life.

In the mid-1800s, European governments, as well as the United States, vied for fur and dried fish that came from various Indigenous Peoples who inhabited the different parts of Alaska. The other governments made treaties among themselves, and they did not consult Alaska's Indigenous Peoples when they did so. Captain Cook came to Alaska looking for an inside passage. The Russians came and treated our Peoples as barbarians and tried to claim sovereignty over our lands and territories. Russia did not claim title and dominion over us. In 1867 the U.S. and Tsarist Russia created the 1867 Treaty of Cession. When the Russian government sold the Russian-American Trading Company to the United States, they did not sell Alaska, and they did not notify those who had dominion over Alaska, the Indigenous Peoples. What the United States bought wasn't Alaska but the quasi-governmental trading rights of the Russian American Trading Companies. Using the legal fiction, they create an illegal order.

Over the many years since the Treaty of Cession, resources have been taken from the state, to the benefit of the U.S. Government, corporations such as oil companies and individual non-Natives, not the Indigenous People. In our area, farmers were brought to the Matanuska Valley in the 1930s and provided lands that were historically and traditionally used by our people. Many of these actions have been in direct conflict with the Sacred Trust the U.S. Government has to protect the social and economic development, religious aspirations, educational advancement, and form of government of the Indigenous Peoples.

In the early 1920s, my great-grandparents Balasculia Stickwan(man) and Frank Nicolai came together. Frank was from the Chiefs at Tarel, where Guggenheim's Syndicate had built a railroad from Cordova to remove a mountain or so of copper. Frank, who was from the Medicine People, moved to his wife's area, upriver from Taral and inland a little. It was the Tyone Lake area, and the Stickwan(man) were known to be a very influential Ahtna family up and down the Copper River, especially in Kluti-Ka, or Copper Center. They roamed from Ahtna to the Knik River Trading Post in the Destnay area. Frank Nicolai had seven brothers, and one moved to Eklutna.

My great-grandparents had relatives at Nay'dini'aa Na' (Chickaloon), including Frank's brothers Bassille and Chicklu, for whom Chickaloon was named. When miners moved to Nay'dini'aa Na', Chiklu relocated across Cook Inlet by Hope. The waters there are now called Chickaloon Bay and River.

One of Frank and Balasculia's daughters, Annie, my grandmother, had 11 children including my dad, Louis Raymond Harrison, Sr. He had seven children. Annie's sisters, Mary and Olga had 14 more of my relatives.

In the mid-1960s my dad attended some meetings, trying to bring us all together. I remember these events because he had won a pool tournament at the Alpine Inn and chose the prize of pop instead of beer, which he took to the meeting. We kids had to wait and look at that pop. It was easy to count, so you couldn't even sneak any. Later my dad was killed, and then the land claims happened. The Alaska Native Claims Settlement Act split family, government, religion, land, resources, fishing and hunting, and children from the Original Peoples. That is Thievery and Genocide.

I was in Kenai in December 1971, living at cousin Patricia Wade's house. Somehow I got shares in Chickaloon-Moose Creek Native Association, Inc., while Patricia got enrolled into Kenai Native Association. Our various other relatives had stock in other villages, while some were not enrolled in any villages and only to their region, and some were enrolled in

"We are only asking for what has been ours for many generations."

— Bobby W. Esai, Sr., 1969

none at all. So we were divided. We were taught all that had transpired was Manifest Destiny, and we were supposed to be corporate now.

But Aunt Angie Stevig, along with several others, registered Chickaloon Village as a Traditional Government with a Council. She passed the scepter to her sister, Helen DePriest, the eldest of Annie's children. During this time I, along with several friends and relatives that included Etok (known by the dominant culture as Charlie Edwardsen, Jr.), Mary Ann Mills, Delice Calcote, Harry Lord, Archie and George Gottschalk, brothers David and Bruce, sister Penny (Harrison) Westing, Cousin Jesse Lanman, Alan Larson, Sr. and his sister Janet, figured out the history that I have related to you. We learned we had governmental rights and ownership that had not been extinguished or taken into account.

Aunt Helen became unable to keep up with this work, so we asked Aunt Katie Wade to be our Elder. She told us to "help our relatives." Aunt Katie didn't start assisting us to earn credit for what she did, but she has earned it along the way. She went to jail with us, fighting for our fishing rights in Kenai. She was with us at the road block in Chickaloon. She has stood by our sides through many other controversial stands that we have taken, including our driver's licenses and vehicle lawsuits, which we have won. The State of Alaska doesn't want to recognize our winning of the lawsuits, but we still won.

I also want to thank all of our Elders, like Aunt Shirley, Uncle Johnny and Paul, who have stood by us and guided us through all these years.

During the time I was checking internationally for our rights and responsibilities as a Sovereign Government my mentor and cousin, Paul Goodlataw, sent me to look at the United Nations and the Organization of American States. He also had me inspect other international instruments to further our rights of Self-Determination and Sovereignty.

In the early 1990s Kari Shaginoff-Johns and I took over and got help from my sister Penny and niece Jenni Harrison (who is now our Executive Director). Through all of this we had many of my cousins, aunts, brothers, and sister on the Council. There are more than I can remember, but I give my sincere "Tsin'aen" (thank you) for all the years. We have gone through pleasure and tears, and we continue to work together.

The Village and I also got involved in International Politics and our Indigenous Rights. We are still involved with the Arctic Athabascan Council as I am the International Chair, with a Permanent Participant seat to Arctic Council, which includes eight countries.

The Cook Inlet Treaty Tribes, consisting of Alaskan villages, has been formed for the purpose of dealing with the corporate intrusion into Tribal affairs.

We have revised our Constitution. I'm not a wordsmith, but we tried to make our laws short and benevolent. Our draft wasn't very short or benevolent, but it was a try and I hoped my relatives would help with this endeavor. I have seen what Cousin Paul Goodlataw and the Indoor Sports Club did to change the face of America for Handicapped Access while he lived in San Francisco. Just think what together we could do to help our Peoples and the Peoples of this world!

The federal government's relationship with Alaska tribes is a continuous and important feature in rural Alaska governance. While this relationship reflects the unique characteristics of Alaska's history, it is rooted in the principle that Alaska Natives are "Indian people" with whom the federal government has a special relationship.

But that doesn't make any of what we do easy. There have been many meetings I have attended where I felt like I was going into a Ku Klux Klan meeting. So often in these sessions, I am limited to five minutes, one minute or even 30 seconds. When I tell sport fisherman that we do not support their "catch and release" because we are not supposed to play with our food, I am speaking a language they do not understand. Even though I am using their own words of English and not my own language of Ahtna Athabascan, they cannot understand many of the concepts that we Indigenous Peoples live by every day.

How can I remind them in 30 seconds what the Elders taught us? We are here to protect and care for the Land. We don't "own" the Land; it owns us. You must begin to realize that exploitation of the Land has reached a limit. If we continue to rape, pillage and plunder the Land, we will have nothing to leave to our children, let alone the seventh generation.

With respect to the Alaska Native Claims Settlement Act, approximately 500 out of about 72,000 Natives who lived in Alaska were given the chance to vote back in 1971. Out of those 500, not only did these people not have legal consent to represent any of the other peoples, but only 300 people actually voted in favor of ANCSA. This act excluded children born after December 18, 1971. This is genocide. Indigenous Peoples of Alaska have never approved of this act.

In 1971, I was in the seventh grade. I was told to join the land claims so that I would get lots of money and land. I went to a meeting. They said it was for us kids' future. Now I am middle age, and my children are grown, and I no longer believe that the settlement act will bring us money and land.

Many attorneys have made their fortunes from ANCSA, and they have gone off and retired. Accountants have retired. Many "managers" have made enough money to retire. The shareholders that the corporations are built on get very little. If our share was just put in a bank account, we would get six times the money. Millions of dollars are still being spent on "management," and yet I'm wondering what will be left for my children.

Government came in and assumed jurisdiction with a promise to protect us from abuse. Government has confiscated our land and resources, sold and leased to oil and other corporations making billions of dollars. If there was a Tribal government structure in Alaska, the corporations would at least have to abide by some of the laws that the tribes set up. What the state is doing is ignoring tribal government status and just working with the corporations.

When we are in disagreement with ANCSA corporations, they label us "dissidents." The corporations haven't been helping the people they're supposed to be helping. We don't have any say when they do the mineral extraction with the multi-nationals that come in, and they're doing this

Dancing at a CIRI Potlatch in 1993 are, from left, Paul Harrison, Dimi Macheras, Billy Pete, Sondra Stewart, Daniel Harrison, and Alex Macheras.

CIRI photo

with the blessings of the state.

When ANCSA was formed, so were 13 regional corporations under the State of Alaska. People were told that if they did not sign up with these corporations they would no longer be considered "Native," and by signing up we would be protecting our hunting and land rights. After people were enrolled into these corporations they were given shares, and that is when the economic genocide began.

When the settlement act originated, the Alaska Natives were supposed to get 2 percent of the royalties from Prudhoe Bay oil fields. To this day the state of Alaska and the federal government are receiving royalties from the Prudhoe Bay oil fields, which have amounted to billions of dollars. Not only are these governments making money on oil, they also make money on the lands they gave us through taxation. It still horrifies me that three decades ago when ANCSA was developed and the People were led to believe we would receive compensation, oppression was a planned event. Today, our People are still some of the poorest in the land. Many of our People are dying on the streets because they have no lands to return to. Natives in Alaska make up about 20 percent of the population, but in jails and mental institutions we are disproportionately represented due to the social conditions inflicted on us by the governments.

We are forced to struggle for simple things like a subsistence lifestyle, even though in Article XII, Section 12, of the State of Alaska Constitution it says that "the state and its people forever disclaim all right or title in or to any property, including fishing rights, and right or title which may be held by or for any Indian, Eskimo or Aleut, or community thereof." We wish to shed light on our People (including the Elders) going to prison for fishing and gathering of our traditional foods. We would like to bring all of these issues to not only the United Nations' attention but also to the people who may be considering a land claims settlement.

At this time, Chickaloon Village and many other Indigenous communities are in litigation to defend our political, economic, social, religious, educational and self-governing rights. We would also like to remind the United

Nations of the Sacred Trust which was said to be paramount to protect us against abuses and insure our just treatment.

The New Year 2000 brought positive changes. We regained ownership of our Sacred Burial Grounds in Sutton, thanks to the CIRI Land Department. Ivan Stickman's remains were laid to rest next to his family in Sutton on February 26. Harry Nicolai's Spirit House was finally placed on his grave after six years. Many prayers and ceremonies were given to welcome the spirits back to our Land that had been held hostage from us for so many years.

Now we are subject to thousands of laws of the United States and the State of Alaska, so many laws, in fact, that no one person can read them all in a lifetime. There are armed state troopers driving around to keep us in line. When we get out of hand they pick us up and say that ignorance of law is no excuse for self-defense. We now go to jail for hunting and fishing.

The United Nations has adopted the legal principle that all peoples have the right of self-determination and right to subsistence in both the International Covenant of Civil and Political Rights and the International Covenant on Economics, Social and Cultural Rights.

The Arctic Policy Report produced in the 1980s by the United States tells how they are using our Indigenous Peoples in their studies and we continue to be used as guinea pigs for the study of cancer, pneumonia and hepatitis B, among other diseases. When we want copies of our health records and studies, we are refused because of national security. We are strong Peoples to have survived the scourges that have devastated our Peoples in Alaska. We have survived flu, smallpox and polio epidemics to mention a few.

The military has left toxic dump waste sites throughout Alaska. Resource extraction has polluted our lands and waters. Now the United States wants to drill in the Arctic National Wildlife Refuge disrupting the survival of the caribou and the Gwich'in Peoples. The United States and the State of Alaska allow multi-national corporations to plunder our wealth and resources. They try to make us believe everyone is benefiting. In fact, several years ago the oil companies celebrated the extraction of 11 billion barrels of oil. With this amount of money every man, woman and child in Alaska could be wealthy. Instead, many people are in poverty, and some are dying on the streets.

We hope and pray that bringing these atrocities to the attention of the world will bring about positive change so our children and our children's children do not have to suffer. I leave you with one message: May Creator Guide Our Footsteps.

We are the People of the Land, the Land is our life, and no one can change that. Tsin'aen.

Carl Marrs

CIRI photo

11. Harnessing business endeavors to achieve Alaska Native goals

By Carl H. Marrs*

Alaska Native Corporations have come a very long way and matured a great deal in the three decades since they were created under the Alaska Native Claims Settlement Act of 1971, known as ANCSA. While many people focus on the fact that this act was an experiment in capitalism on a grand scale, what I would like to stress is that the designers of the experiment were Alaska's indigenous people. What they sought – and achieved – was an act of self-determination.

As a matter of fact, ANCSA was really the first real settlement between Native Americans and the federal government that was an act of self-determination. The previous treaties and settlements involved land and assets held in trust for Native people by the government and controlled by the Bureau of Indian Affairs. Under ANCSA, the 44 million acres of land and the $1 billion granted to Alaska Natives were controlled by Native boards of directors of Native corporations.

Thirty years after they were created, Alaska Native Corporations have become powerful economic engines with a profound effect on the Alaska economy. Business endeavors run the gamut in Alaska from real estate and natural resource development to construction, tourism and retail operations. Additionally, many of the corporations have invested in a wide range of businesses outside of Alaska. The corporations' importance and influence continue to grow at an exponential rate, giving them a powerful political voice in the state. At the same time, the corporations concern themselves with the social needs of Alaska Natives, as well as their economic well-being.

First published in Cultural Survival Quarterly, Fall 2003 issue

Although Alaska Native Corporations are businesses in every sense of the word, there are some unique differences between them and other corporations in Alaska. For one thing, the leaders of the regional corporations work together as a team in many arenas, including the Association of ANCSA Regional Corporation Presidents/CEOs. This organization was created to foster leadership and teamwork among Native leaders. Because I am so familiar with my fellow corporate leaders, I am intimately aware that although we are all Native corporations, the way we go about achieving Native goals and objectives differs.

CIRI has done extremely well over the years, in part because our board has focused on stability for the long term. Throughout most of our history, we have decided against paying out a large percentage of our capital, despite sometimes fervent voices urging us to do just that. Other corporations have at times found this force among their shareholders to be immutable, and some directors have found themselves forced off their boards in favor of new directors who are less concerned about growing their corporation.

And yet, we at CIRI have had less time to focus attention on important issues like subsistence that are so very vital in other regions, such as the NANA Region in Northwest Alaska or the Arctic Slope Region and many others. Early on, NANA and Doyon decided that creation of jobs for shareholders was a high priority, and they have done a very commendable job of doing just that. Arctic Slope Regional Corp. has opted to focus on the development of revenue, and they are succeeding, too.

In fact, it is my belief that all of our corporations are just now beginning to come into their own and that we'll see a lot more success throughout Alaska as a result. In order to reach this point, many of us, as with most corporations in America, have had hard times. Sometimes there are economic factors beyond our control. But the true test of management is to work through the hard times and turn the losses around over time.

My fellow CEO's work hard at achieving the very best for the Native people of Alaska, and while all of us are taking somewhat different paths

Margie Brown, CIRI President and CEO, is shown in this 1990 photo with George Miller, the corporation's first president.

May 26, 1919 – Birth of George Miller, Jr.

Kenaitze leader George Miller, Jr., was born May 26, 1919, in the now abandoned village of Stepanka near the outlet of Skilak Lake on the Kenai Peninsula to Fiona Mishakoff, a traditional Dena'ina healer and midwife and German immigrant George Miller. Miller became the first president of Cook Inlet Region, Inc., and later focused his energy on establishing the Kenai Natives Association to represent the Kenaitze people.

Miller was an outspoken advocate for Alaska Native rights, and he was among many Alaska Natives who lobbied for and testified in favor of settling Alaska Native land claims in congressional hearings that eventually led to passage of the Alaska Native Claims Settlement Act of 1971. Miller successfully advocated on behalf of urban Natives of the Kenai and Anchorage areas to ensure that they would not be left out of the settlement.

He was elected interim president of CIRI in 1972, serving as an unpaid volunteer, and helped

toward that goal, we are all working to better Native people socially and economically. Knowing that gives me great respect for my fellow CEO's. The dignity they bring to their efforts has led to many remarkable success stories that are only beginning to be written throughout Alaska.

When I reflect upon the sweeping changes that have been made in Alaska's political, economic and social landscape as a result of ANCSA and the creation of Native corporations, I find myself turning to our Native Elders. I appreciate their wisdom more and more, especially as I rapidly approach becoming an Elder.

As Native corporations, we are expending an ever-increasing amount of energy on the spiritual well-being of our people. Our Elders have taught us that we are people who are part of something larger than we are. This intangible quality makes it most difficult for non-Natives to understand just what it is that Native corporations are about. Native corporations were created as the embodiment of a desire to craft a settlement "in conformity with the real economic and social needs of Natives." I've cited those words on a number of occasions, and I continue to look to them because they explain in simple language what we are about.

In addition to the nearly 200 Alaska Native Corporations operating in Alaska, there are dozens of Native organizations, non-profit organizations and other entities that are a direct result of ANCSA. Altogether, these many entities provide a great deal of shelter to many people. The corporations created under ANCSA are looking to the long-term future in creating institutions that may well live long after the corporations. These include local housing authorities, health agencies and other social service organizations, foundations which in many cases are generously endowed and statewide facilities such as the Alaska Native Heritage Center.

At the same time, some Native corporations have been able to seize hold of key opportunities. ASRC was the first Native corporation to make the Forbes 500 list in the 1990's, after Sealaska's listing in the mid-1980's. CIRI, while smaller in gross revenues, has shown consistently strong earnings. Among Alaskan businesses, Native corporations most likely are the largest importers of profits to Alaska. Some of our biggest business enterprises are Outside. But while we do business in the Lower 48 and throughout the world, we're committed to Alaska. We'll bring the money back, wherever the profits are made.

The Association of ANCSA Regional Corporation Presidents/CEOs for the last three years has sponsored a statewide survey and report on the overall economic impact of Native corporations on the state. The most recent report includes data from the year 2001 for the 13 regional corporations and 30 of the 168 village corporations operating in the state.

The report shows that Native corporations provide jobs, revenue, and commitment to the Alaska economy. Some key highlights for the 43 corporations surveyed include:

- Revenue of $2.9 billion and assets of $2.9 billion.
- $52.1 million in dividends and $434 million in payroll (within Alaska).
- Statewide employment of 13,062.
- Alaska Native employment of 3,122.
- $9.3 million donated to charitable organizations and $4.1million distributed for scholarships to 2,821 recipients.

Such substantial contributions to charities in Alaska, as well as scholarships for Alaska Native students, and dividends for Native corporation shareholders provide a glimpse of the very significant impact Native corporations have on the Alaska economy.

Of the 43 corporations included in the report, 13 were recognized by *Alaska Business Monthly* (October 2002) as among the state's top 49 most successful Alaskan businesses. The list was led by Arctic Slope Regional Corporation. Five Native regional corporations were in the top 10, and eight other Native regional and village corporations also made the list.

The report notes that 2001 had mixed financial results for the corporations overall, but it was a record year for CIRI. Net income was more than four times the previous year's amount. This was driven largely by the sale of CIRI's telecommunications investments with VoiceStream Wireless

develop the first budget for CIRI. From its first $130,000 budget, CIRI grew and developed into one of the more successful of the 12 in-state Native regional corporations. After the CIRI board was formed, Miller stepped down as president in 1973. He was elected president of the Kenai Natives Association, where he served for 13 years. In part as a result of his efforts, the association secured the former Wildwood Air Force Base, which comprised nearly 4,300 acres of land as well as buildings, furnishing and paved one-way streets. The association developed an educational facility for Native students and housing for Alaska Natives at the site and later sold the former base to the state for a prison.

"You are now on Indian land," Miller said on March 28, 1974, in a ceremony to mark the transfer of the land from the federal government to the Kenai Natives Association. He died on Oct. 23, 1996, in Soldotna.

Kenaitze Chief Rika Murphy, who died in 1990, worked closely with Miller in the 1960s and 1970s. Her daughter, Hazel Felton, described Miller as a tireless advocate for his people. "He was a kind and gentle man with a fiery spirit," Felton said.

- June 6, 2004

Corporation, which we view as a one-time "home-run" that we were able to pass on to our shareholders in special distributions of nearly $400 million.

Total net income for the 13 regional corporations combined in 2001 was $455 million, which was offset by net losses of $36 million sustained by five of the corporations. The total equity in 2001 was $1.5 billion.

Yet, as we celebrate our successes, we can't forget that despair continues to nip at the heels of many of our family members. Many Alaska Natives who work at CIRI volunteer their time to assist at Bean's Café in Anchorage and many other charities throughout the city. But the fact remains that many of the people who need the services of these agencies most are also Alaska Natives, though there has been vast improvement since 1971.

As Native corporation leaders, we continue to ask ourselves how the power and the profits of Native corporations can best be harnessed to empower our people and honor our cultures. When we look to the past, we see that the Native leadership was instrumental in crafting ANCSA to create an act of self-determination. The goal was not the creation of reservations, but a new kind of business enterprise controlled in every way by Alaska Natives.

These business enterprises have succeeded and are thriving. ANCSA has become the biggest minority success story of the nation. The act did not solve all the social problems of Alaska's Native people, but it was never intended to solve all the problems.

As we look to the future, we can look to our cultural and traditional values and our Elders for guidance. The leaders who crafted ANCSA wisely developed an evolving agreement, which has been amended many times in its history and likely will be amended many more times in the future. Those who will make the changes in the future will be Native people themselves – in an act of self-determination.

12. Our future will be shaped by our cultural knowledge

By Aaron Leggett

Aaron Leggett
CIRI photo

For the last several years, I have heard how my contemporaries and I are the future of the Alaska Native world. This idea is hard to grasp. The reason I say this is because for most of my life I never really gave much thought to the fact that I was Alaska Native. My two younger siblings Adam and Angela and I grew up in Anchorage in what felt like a pretty "normal" middle class life – my mom, Diane, was a stay-at-home mother, and my father, Rick, worked for the Alaska Railroad. I had some knowledge about my Native background, such as that my maternal grandmother was from Eklutna and that through her, we were Dena'ina Athabascan.

And yet, on the rare occasion when I thought about the fact that I was Native, it seemed negative, not positive. There was – and still is – an undercurrent of racism in Anchorage, and I mainly dealt with it by denial.

My first job, while I was in high school, was working for Southcentral Foundation, the Native non-profit health entity for CIRI, our Native region-al corporation. At the time, I didn't really understand the significance of it, but as I grew older I realized the experience that I gained gave me my first insights into the world of Alaska Native issues. I then went two summers outside of the Native community, including a stint at the Alaska Railroad as a tour guide. It wasn't until I started working at the Alaska Native Heritage Center when was I was 19 that I really started focusing on what it means to be an Alaska Native. When I first started working at the heritage center I told myself that I wanted to do things that were more tourism-related and less focused on the Native cultural aspect. I believe I did that because I was scared – scared that no one would want to hear what I had to say. In the back of my mind lurked the fear that somehow I wasn't a "true" Native.

Maybe I felt guilty about my denial, and maybe I feared that I'd have nothing to say to the tourists.

I soon realized, however, that I enjoyed the cultural aspect. I was fascinated by it. As I learned more about my culture, I started to learn more about myself. For the first time, I started to understand who I am. I was able to let go of my misconception that being "only" a quarter Athabascan somehow made me "less" of a Native.

While working at the Alaska Native Heritage Center I could not help but begin taking pride in who I am. The price of admission told a story in itself. People were paying 20 dollars each to come and learn about Alaska's first people. But it was the other employees who really got my attention. For the first time I started to meet people who were my age and of similar backgrounds but also were Native and proud of it.

While I was growing up, identifying myself as "Native" did not bring to mind a heritage of pride. There wasn't any talk about the Dena'ina culture, stretching back hundreds of years, and I knew little if anything about our oral traditions. All I knew was that it was humiliating when my father's insurance company dropped its dental care plan and my siblings and I had to go to the old Native hospital on Third Avenue, then known as the Alaska Native Services hospital. Entering that building was like a slap in the face. I could almost hear a voice saying, "Well, Aaron, here you are. You can't hide your Native heritage forever." And as I started to walk through there, I would feel more and more ashamed of being Native. It seemed like this is what the government said being Native is worth. It's only worth us having this hospital that was at its prime years before I was even born, and had since become quite outdated.

I know that I am not the only one who felt this way. I have talked with many people my age, and they have all said basically the same thing, that it wasn't a place that any of them liked to go to.

Growing up, I guess I was sort of stuck in the middle. I wanted to be able to claim my Native heritage, but I didn't know much about it and I also wanted to blend in like everyone else. It bothered me every time I heard someone say something like, "Well, if Natives want to hunt, they should be required to hunt the traditional way." I felt disgusted when they'd say: "All Natives do is get checks each month and spend them on booze." It wasn't so much that it hurt me, but when they said that I thought about my mom or grandmother and that maybe that's what people thought of them.

I do understand that alcohol and drug abuse is a serious problem within the Native community throughout Alaska. But as I grow older I realize that things like living in a community where there aren't many jobs can be demoralizing. And maybe some of this behavior stems from a sense of hopelessness that even runs through generations. I've heard the theories about a genetic base to these problems. But that's hard for me to accept: How do you explain the fact that Alaska Natives commit suicide at three to four times the rate among White Americans throughout the country? Or how about the fact that Alaska Natives comprise only about 19 percent of the population of Alaska, but about 38 percent of all inmates are Alaska Natives, according to a 2004 report by the Alaska Native Policy Center. I don't think it's because we are more violent or that we are more depressed. I feel it is because of social inequality that we have faced in the past and continue to deal with to this day.

What I learned from my public education was that Natives were something to be studied. Their day had past. If the cultures were still around, they were on the verge of dying out. The only positive things about the cultures were things that Western culture appreciated such as Southeast Native artwork with its elaborate designs and carvings. The thing is, I either got only part of the story, or I got it wrong altogether.

I can remember being in the fourth grade. We had to write a short paper on how Athabascans used bear spears. What they didn't tell us was that in Athabascan cultures, bears have a very powerful spirit that is easily offended. We never learned that it was only men who hunted bears, nor did we find out that it was a major undertaking with up to a month of preparation. The hunter has to follow a set of rules including not allowing women to know about the hunt. They would never say that they were going bear hunting for this was taboo. Instead they might say something like: I am going to visit my friend in the woods.

When I think back to my school experiences, I'm angry about the fact that I got so little of the real story. I remember when my fourth grade teacher read us a story one day after lunch. It was the winter, and in my mind I can still see that my classmates' cheeks were still rosy red from playing outside at recess. We all sat on the carpet and listened to her start to read a story out loud. I don't recall her saying that the book was *Tanaina Tales*, by Bill Vaudin. But even if she had, I know she didn't say the "Tanaina," now known as Dena'ina, were the people who lived in Anchorage and Cook Inlet before the railroad came in 1914. It wasn't until 10 years later that I realized that the story she was reading was from my people, my grandmother and her ancestors to be exact. My teacher didn't read the whole story. She thought all the violence was inappropriate for us. She quit reading to us halfway through, but not before she clearly expressed her disgust. It's too bad she didn't do her own homework and read the story in advance. If she had had a better grounding in my culture, it would have helped her see that the violence was meant to teach a lesson.

Things haven't changed much in the Anchorage School District. In 1997 a Chugiak High School teacher assigned a Native American story from the book *American Indians and Legends*, edited by Richard Erdoes and Alfonso Ortitz to his class of high school juniors. He had not read the story before assigning it, and it was later deemed to be too sexually explicit for high school students. He was suspended for three days without pay and barely escaped being fired. The book itself was later banned from the district, one of only three books to be banned in the last 20 years.

While there are those who might suggest that these teachers deserve some credit for attempting to focus on Native stories, doing so in such a superficial manner and without any context is actually worse than nothing at all. While I was growing up, not once did we ever have an actual Alaska Native come into our schools and provide information about his or her culture. Strangely, we did learn a lot about other cultures from visiting artists who came from places like Japan and Mexico. And then there was the artist, Robin Heller from Philadelphia, whose comic strip "Mukluk" poked "fun" at Inupiaq people. As I think back to his visit to our class, it's disturbing to realize that we never had a presentation from an Inupiaq person. I guess in the spirit of fairness, I'm not terribly upset that Heller spoke to us because his comic strip was rather benign or even banal, but even so, there should have been a balance.

As I started to learn more about Alaska Natives, I began to get a sense of what it must have been like for my grandmother to make trips to Anchorage from Eklutna when she was a young girl. It would have probably been impossible for her to avoid seeing the signs that said "No Natives or Dogs" in the 1930s and 1940s. Neither my mother nor my grandmother ever discussed any of this with me. My theory is that Grandma set up a defense mechanism that served her throughout her life, a defense mechanism that she, in fact, passed on to my mother. Grandma gave the impression that being Native wasn't anything special. She never really had time to be Native or share much of what she grew up with. I'm ashamed to say, as a kid I was proud of the fact that my grandmother acted so "white." She didn't act "Native" or talk with an accent. At her house, we never ate moose meat or anything like that. In fact, when I was working at the Alaska Native Heritage Center if people asked me what I learned from my grandmother, I used to tell them I learned how to play bingo and the starting lineup to the Atlanta Braves.

Today, I understand that in her lifetime, my grandmother saw Anchorage grow to be a big city, a place that no longer valued the things she was taught. When her grandfather took her sheep hunting, they stayed at his cabin near the head of Eklutna Lake. But those days are gone. The cabin, now rented out to hikers, is controlled by Chugach State Park. Sheep hunting is outlawed.

As I grow older I realize my grandmother was a woman of great strength. She knew she could not give me the sheep hunting that her grandfather gave her. She could not give me Eklutna Lake, at least not in

"Most people do not believe that the Indians had developed title to their land or ties with the land. This is completely misconceived because land and the Indians were bound together by ties of kinship and nature rather than by an understanding of property ownership. This conception is the very essence of Indian life. . .
"A nation which was founded on the principles of freedom and justice has violated its own principles."

— Charles Etok Edwardsen, Jr., 1968

a literal way. Because of all that she had to deal with, too much of her focus was on basic dignity. I'm proud of what she taught me, though, because I believe she found a way to tell me she was proud of me. In a way I think she was happy to see that it had become acceptable to learn about and want to know about Athabascan customs and such. I know that as long as she lived, she was proud that I wanted to learn more. In fact, I believe it was a relief to her that our heritage wasn't going to die with her.

And speaking of death, my village of Eklutna is probably best known for our cemetery, Eklutna Historical Park, which has what are called "spirit houses" on each of the graves. These spirit houses are a blending of Native custom and Russian Orthodoxy. After the Dena'ina were converted to orthodoxy, we could no longer cremate our dead so we built these small structures, giving the spirits a place to stay for 40 days until they made their final journey.

Since it was only 20 miles from Anchorage, over the years many people have visited the cemetery. But the ultimate irony is that the descendents of the people who are buried there don't even own the land on which the original cemetery is located and do not have ultimate authority to make decisions about that property. My feelings about our cemetery bring me full circle back to the statement that I am a future leader. It's an honor to have such a title but at the same time it can be rather frightening.

I, Aaron Leggett, a kid who was diagnosed with a learning disability, do want to help my people. If that means running a billion-dollar corporation, so be it. If it means fighting for the right to make decisions about my grandmother's final resting place and even my mother's and other members of my family, so be it.

At the same time, I feel strongly pulled in another direction. For a long time, I told myself that I wasn't going to be able to learn the language and even if I did what would I do with it? Out of the 1,000 Dena'ina Athabascans living today, probably only 75 of us can still speak the language. Luckily, much has been recorded and preserved so the information is sitting waiting to be used. Over a weekend in June 2004 I drove down to Kenai, and went to a Dena'ina festival. While I was there I started to realize that maybe I should reexamine what I want to do in life. Maybe the way that I might be able to best help my people is to study the language and at least learn how to read and write it. At this conference I realized that if I don't step up to the plate and do something about this then who will? I realized that none of the speakers are getting any younger and in fact one of our Elders passed away over that weekend. When I heard that news I started to realize what an opportunity I had lost by not taking advantage of learning from him what I could when I was able to.

In June 2005, I went to Kenai and spent three weeks learning our language at the Dena'ina Language Institute. While I was there I had the opportunity to spend a lot of time with several Elders including Andrew Balluta, a renowned Elder from Nondalton who helped write a book on our people with Linda Ellana.

I will never forget some of the conversations and insights that he shared with me. One night during a gathering he and I both told several stories. What made this so special is that he later told me how much he enjoyed it. He said it reminded him of how they used to go back and forth and see who could tell the best story. If they missed something, someone would correct them. It was the first time I had ever told Dena'ina stories in front of a predominantly Dena'ina audience. I'll always remember seeing the faces as I spoke to the group; their reaction told me I hit the mark and that they enjoyed it.

The day before we left several Elders told stories in our language. One of the stories was the Chickadee story I heard when I was in school that my teacher hated and thought was so disgusting. Sitting by that I fire, I felt powerfully that I knew exactly what they were talking about. I didn't understand every word they spoke, but they conveyed to me what this story is about and why it is important to our culture. The people who lived long before wanted us to get the message: sometimes the right way is counterintuitive. We can't allow ourselves to be blinded by our preconceptions about what's right and what's wrong.

Fred Bismark
*The CIRI
Foundation photo*

April 6, 1923 – Birth of Tyonek leader Frederick T. Bismark

Dena'ina village leader and commercial fisherman Frederick "Fred" Theodore Bismark of Tyonek, who played an instrumental role in financing lobbying efforts for the Alaska Native Claims Settlement Act, was born April 6, 1923, in Anchorage. When he was about 10 years old, his family moved to Tyonek, across Cook Inlet from Anchorage, and Bismark spent most of the rest of his life in the village.

The Dena'ina Athabascan residents of the village of Tyonek sued for and received proceeds of $12 million from a 1964 oil lease sale for 25,000 acres of the village's reservation land. Later, they received an additional $2.7 million from a second sale. Villagers used the money for road and airstrip improvements and health and welfare projects, as well as housing for villagers. As a result of their well thought out plan of expending their funds, they became a model cited on numerous occasions during congressional hearings on the Alaska Native Claims Settlement Act in the late 1960s.

Besides using the money within the village, villagers generously shared some of their revenue

Through my job at CIRI and Cook Inlet Tribal Council, I have met many of the leaders in the Native community who helped create and shape the Alaska Native Claims Settlement Act of 1971. These are people such as Willie Hensley, Roy Huhndorf, Byron Mallott, Trefon Angasan and John Shively just to name a few. I have also been privileged to meet people who have studied my culture, people such as Alan Boraas, James Kari, Jim Fall or Nancy Yaw Davis. And the big question is, do I go down the corporate path or do I try and do something that relates to the degree I am pursuing in Anthropology and pick up where others have left off? I'm not saying that if I do one I cannot do the other, it is just that I believe that I am going to have to find a balance because I feel that without the cultural aspect our corporations are nothing special. But also I feel that I have learned too much already in the last few years with regard to ANCSA including doing research for this book that I do want to be able to help in some way to give my perspective to some type of Alaska Native business.

Since I was born in 1981 instead of 1971 I am in a category that some have labeled "afterborns" or "new Natives." Unlike our parents, many people my age are not shareholders in any corporation. Although I have received shares from my grandmother's estate, many of my contemporaries have not inherited stock. For all of us, it is not a sure thing. I could have been left out of the corporation because someone in my family liked one of my siblings more than me. Before I became a shareholder in my village corporation and my regional corporation, I sometimes felt my ideas did not count for as much.

As Alaska Natives we should be on the same field and all have 100 shares. In other words, what is the incentive for board members now serving to listen to someone who doesn't have the right to vote on corporation matters? It's possible that permanent damage could have already been done to the company by the time younger people get a chance to voice their opinions.

So what should be done? Native corporations should open up the books and add Alaska Natives born after 1971, as has already been done by three Native regional corporations and some village corporations. ANCSA wasn't about one generation. It's about all Alaska Natives. If my corporation decided to sell off all its land, it would be robbing me, my future. And that's something that can't be measured in dollars. It would be selling a tie to the land that has been a part of our culture for well over 12,000 years. I pray that in my lifetime I never have to face the fact that all our land is gone and all we have is a corporation which has capital and no land. Without the land, how are our Native corporations any different from any other corporation?

What I propose is that all the corporations be opened up and younger Alaska Natives be added as shareholders. There is a danger that this could lead to smaller dividends for all shareholders, but we need to understand, it's not about the money. It's about our birthright and the land.

There could be a problem with younger shareholders – the same problem we have right now with some older shareholders – and that is shareholders who are overly concerned about the size of their dividends. And finally, there is a concern that if people are too far removed from Alaska Native issues, by virtue of distance or of a tie to the Native Community, that they will favor policy decisions that are not in the best interest of Alaska Natives in the future. This leads me to the idea that all students in the state of Alaska should have a much greater understanding of what Alaska Native Corporations are all about. If this type of information were taught within our schools, people would start to realize that Alaska Natives – united Alaska Natives – are by far the single most powerful group in Alaska. The fact that we own 92 percent of all fee simple land in the state of Alaska should tell you something. Teaching kids at a young age about their heritage will lead to greater self esteem.

Sometimes it's hard for me to believe that I am really here, working for my Native corporation. Sometimes I have to remind myself how lucky I am. How many 24-year-olds work for a company worth several hundred million dollars? How many 24-year-olds are part owners of such a company? But it is more than money. As I walk around our building, it's the little things that

with the newly formed Alaska Federation of Natives. Bismark was vice president of the village council when the council voted to assist AFN in its lobbying efforts.

Bismark discussed how the villagers decided to use their money in an oral history interview in Our Stories, Our Lives, published by The CIRI Foundation in 1986 and re-issued in 2002. Besides talking about his life in general, he discussed the fact that the villagers wanted to do as much research as possible before they expended any of their oil funds.

"Before we got into spending money, they sent me on a tour. I've been to New Mexico, Old Mexico, Arizona, Colorado, Oklahoma, California, Washington, Kansas, District of Columbia, Cleveland, Chicago.

"I think I covered just about all the states, looking at all the Indian reservations to see where they made their mistakes and see where they made good investments," he said.

Bismark died on Jan. 10, 2000, in Anchorage and was buried in Tyonek Cemetery.

- April 4, 2004

157

one starts to notice. Take, for example, CIRI's extensive Native art collection. It's an inspiration to work in a place that celebrates Native artists. We have pieces from well established artists, and we have some from relatively unknown artists. We have pieces that are purely decorative, and some that are functional. We have art that is only a few years old, and we have artifacts that are several hundred years old. As I walk around and look at the pieces in CIRI's collection, I realize that in many ways our corporation is a link to the past. It's also a link to the future.

Another example of what makes CIRI different is that fact that as I sit down to write this piece, I smell smoked salmon strips. To me, that smell of delicious food is a further reminder that we, as an ANCSA corporation, are different. It's a good feeling to hear people discussing the finer points of smoked salmon – is it too smokey? Too oily? Just right? Our corporations show that we don't have to give up being Native to be successful in life. We can be proud of who we are, and there is nothing wrong with eating smoked salmon strips at 9 in the morning. When we eat smoked salmon, we're going beyond feeding our stomachs. We're also honoring my ancestors, maybe even connecting to them, even if it is for just that brief moment. While the technology for catching the fish has changed, little else in the way they are processed has in the last several thousand years. And most importantly, it isn't just the fact that people are going out to get food for their families, it's the activity itself that is so important. It's a way to connect to the past. It doesn't matter whether it is done with guns or nets or gas boats. It's being able to get out into the landscape of our ancestors and do something that has been done for thousands of years.

I get angry when I hear someone say that they support subsistence so long as Natives use traditional methods. I would ask that person what is traditional? Is it using dog sleds instead of snowmachines? And yet, it wasn't until the Russians came in that Alaska Natives started to use dogs to pull sleds. Or how about using a fishwheel instead of nylon nets? The fishwheel didn't show up until about 1900. My point is that for ten thousand years the people of Alaska adapted through innovations that made things easier. Why would it be now that we aren't allowed to adapt again and take advantage of what is available? We should not have to give up our activities because we have access to new technologies.

So my hope in writing this chapter is to show that many Alaska Natives struggle with identity. Whether it be in the boardroom of a billion-dollar corporation or living day-to-day in a village, Alaska Natives are constantly asking themselves who they are and how best to fit into the world around us? Some of us spend part of our lives trying to hide our most basic identity. This is sad, and it's wrong, and I believe spreading the message of who we are as Alaska's first people is one way to combat that. Having people embrace all our unique cultures will lead to higher self-esteem. Alaska Natives don't have to give up who we are to be successful in life.

I am reminded every day of the wisdom of many elders. Their message is: "Take the best of both worlds and use all that is available to us to succeed in life." In the end we, as Alaska Natives, will benefit from this. We, as a state and a country, can learn to better understand and respect those values and beliefs that make each group unique. We will all be better people when we recognize that there are valuable contributions that have been made to Alaska and will continue to be made as long as there are people willing to try to understand Alaska's first inhabitants.

Sheri Buretta
Chugach Alaska Corp. photo

13. Epilogue

By Sheri Buretta

First, who we are. . .we are Inupiaq, Yup'ik, Cup'ik, Siberian Yupik, Tlingit, Haida, Tsimshian, Eyak, Athabascan, Aleut, and Alutiiq. We are the indigenous people of Alaska. For over 10,000 years our ancestors have lived and thrived in one of the harshest areas of the world. We are the last remaining indigenous people in the United States to have never been forcibly removed from our homelands and settled in reservations. We have more than 230 small villages scattered in the largest land mass contained in one state of the union. The residents of many of these Native villages depend on subsistence hunting and fishing to sustain their bodies as well as their traditions and cultures.

In 1960, over 64 percent of our people lived on incomes below the federal poverty level. By 1970, 39 percent of Alaska Natives lived below the federal poverty level. In 1971, our land claims were settled, and we embarked on a new course, integrating ourselves into the cash economy with corporate structures to build an economic base for our people.

We are encouraged to say the poverty rate has been reduced to 20 percent, but there are still disparities between Alaska Natives and other Alaskans that deserve focused attention. We are very proud of the collective efficiency of our Alaska Native Corporations to improve the lives of our people.

In 1971, the United States Congress settled the land claims of Alaska's Native people utilizing the corporate structure to manage both the land and the case. It was considered a great experiment in capitalism, providing a basis to develop economic self-sufficiency.

Our Alaska Native Corporations, known as ANCs, have matured a great deal in the last 34 years. ANCs have become the main vessel for our people to compete in the marketplace. They are the economic engines charged with creating economic value and opportunities in our homelands, employing our people, and supporting social and cultural programs important to our people. ANCs also are engaged in the larger economic arena to capture new technologies, build greater capacities in management and labor, and transform the way we do business.

While each ANC is unique, we strive to work together, cooperating on key issues affecting Alaska indigenous people. The traditional model provided to us by our Elders is one knowing that the needs of the group take precedence over the need of the individual. It is this key difference that many people outside of the Alaska Native community find so difficult to understand. As Alaska Natives, we never forget that each one of us is part of something larger than ourselves. It is this knowledge that has brought all of us together, even groups that many years ago were traditional enemies.

As an example, the leaders of the Alaska Native regional corporations work together as a team in many arenas, including the Association of ANCSA Regional Corporation Presidents and CEOs. This organization was created to foster leadership and teamwork among Native leaders, and it is with great humility that I have accepted the position of president of this organization. I am the first woman to hold this position, and I am following in the footsteps of Carl Marrs, former President/CEO of Cook Inlet Region, Inc. He is a leader for whom I have the highest regard. I know that all of our work is of vital importance to Alaska Natives and the entire state as well.

Our focus this year is on Government Contracting because we believe there is a great deal of misunderstanding of Alaska Native Corporations in general. We participate in the federal contracting marketplace through one key method: the Small Business Administration's 8(a) program. By statute and regulation, the 8(a) Program allows our companies to develop businesses over time by building expertise through government contracts. Given that we have hundreds (and often thousands) of owners or members of each Tribe or Alaska Native Corporation, the profits we earn are dispersed over a wider group of people than in a typical 8(a) company. We do this because we were created by the U.S. Congress to have a dual

"Malrugni Yuuluni/Walking in Two Worlds With One Spirit" is the fifth annual report on the economic impact of Alaska Native Corporations on the Alaska economy. It is published by the Association of ANCSA Regional Corporation Presidents/CEOs.
Photo courtesy Association of ANCSA Regional Corporation Presidents/CEOs.

responsibility, to provide for our people's social and economic needs and build for them a sustainable future. It is an enormous undertaking that is still progressing.

This 8(a) Program is helping us to bring economic self-sufficiency to our people, many of whom still live in Third World conditions, lacking the most basic amenities of even sewer and water. We are building our businesses for one key reason: to improve the lives of our Tribal members and Alaska Native Corporation shareholders. The federal government has a special trust relationship with Native Americans and the indigenous people of Alaska. It is rooted in the U.S. Constitution wherein Congress is granted authority to regulate commerce with the Tribes. Two hundred years of court cases have strongly affirmed this trust relationship and congressional responsibility. Nonetheless, the Federal Government's numerous attempts to work with or assist the Native populations have often fallen terribly short of expectations. The government contracting rules that help us are an obvious exception to those failures. The good news is that Alaska Native Corporations and other Tribal organizations are showing success in doing exactly what Congress intended, finally building sustainable businesses that train our people return a profit to our owners, educate Native children and push our communities out of poverty.

The Alaska Native Corporation story is an incredible story we are very happy to share.

– Reprinted with permission from Malrugni Yuuluni, *Walking in Two Worlds With One Spirit*, 2005, Association of ANCSA

APPENDIX

"THE LAND IS THE SPIRIT OF THE PEOPLE"
KEYNOTE SPEECH
BY WILLIE HENSLEY
AFN CONVENTION
ANCHORAGE, ALASKA – OCTOBER 23, 1980

▨ Introduction

Chairman Jack, President Ferguson, Ladies and Gentlemen: I would like to tell you how honored I am to be speaking to you, and I would like to thank the Board of Directors of the Alaska Federation of Natives for asking me to make the keynote address.

This is the 14th annual convention of the Alaska Federation of Natives. I would like to know how many of you were here in 1966 for the first convention. Those of you who might have been here in Anchorage then, would you please stand?

. . .Now that the rest of you see who they are, you know who is responsible for all the problems we've had the last several years. . .If you have a gripe or a complaint, about this section or that section of the Alaska Native Claims Settlement Act, you can go to them and tell them about it.

Native land rights are the major issue of our time and the AFN was created in 1966 to address the problems of our rights to our land. We all know that the Settlement Act of 1971 is not perfect, but we also know that it is the major legislation shaping the Native community today. As I prepared to speak to you this morning, my thoughts were centered on the Settlement Act.

Thanks

First, I would like to thank the Tyonek Indian people. Some of you who are new or very young may not know that it was that group which really was responsible for most of us being financially able to get to Anchorage in October of 1966 when we first met. Most of us didn't have the finances then to get together for a meeting about our lands, but the Tyonek Indians had just received royalty payments for gas and oil explorations. They could have been satisfied to have their own needs met, but they generously made funding available to press for a settlement for other Native people. I would like to hear a little applause for them because they stuck their necks out at a time when the odds were against their ever being repaid for their financial contribution.

Also there is one person in particular that I think we owe a great deal to, and I would like to thank him and the organization that he headed. The Cook Inlet Native Association was the host for the first AFN convention and the person who headed C.I.N.A. at that time and who had the nerve to get up and take the leadership of AFN was Emil Notti. Some of you do not understand, I think, that it took quite a little bit of guts in those days to try to say what we knew all along: that is, that we owned the land.

We also owe thanks to the traditional leaders – the real leadership – of the Native communities. Even as recently as the 1960's, the atmosphere in Alaska was intimidating and made it difficult to speak for land rights. In those days, many Native people were afraid to come from their villages to talk about the land, but they came in and spoke anyway. You should look at the 1968 hearing record, when Senator Jackson brought his committee up here. It took courage and foresight for our traditional leaders to speak as they did and we can be proud of them. We've come a long way since 1966 simply because we put aside our historical and cultural differences and were able to move with unity.

Why the Land?

Although we've had a major influence on Alaska – how it is now and how it's going to be in the future – there's a great deal of confusion as to what we have created. I think there are many people – many of our own people – who do not understand why we fought so hard for the land.

Basically, we did not fight for the land because it represented capital, or because it represented money, or because it represented business opportunities. We fought for the land because it represents the spirit of our people. It represents your tribes and it represents your ancestors and it represents that intimate knowledge of the land that your people grew up on for ten thousand years. And when we fought for the land, we really were fighting for survival – not economic survival, or political survival, but survival as a people with an identity – people with a culture.

The land is the spirit of our people. It is the home of the spirits of our ancestors. By the 1960's, the land was all we really had left for maintaining our identity. Our rights to the land were not yet confirmed, and by 1966 we were in danger of losing all that we had left: that was the land. We knew that we had to fight for the land. This is where we were in 1966 when Native people came together for the first time as a united people at the first convention of the Alaska Federation of Natives. Five years later we had a land settlement.

Unlike the American Indians in the "Lower 48" who fought in the mountains and in the valleys and in the deserts, the battleground we fought on was political. We fought the battles (with very few troops) in alien soil – in the Congress, in the legislature, in the press, on television, and at the podiums. We did not control that battlefield, but we fought hard, in effect, with broken bows and broken lances, and it's important for the young people to know that.

The Settlement

Why we fought for a settlement should be understood, if our main objective of survival is to be achieved. What I mean by survival is not just economic survival, or political survival. I'm talking about our original goal of the survival of our tribal spirit, of our languages, our culture and our self-respect. We should not be confused. The Settlement Act must be analyzed in light of two hundred years of American history – the end product of an effort to de-Indianize the Native population. The land we won – the land which represents our spiritual homeland – now rests in the corporation: a soulless entity that is designed for commercial purpose.

As you know, this was not a usual settlement. The Indians in the "Lower 48" had tribes and tribal governments that were responsible for the survival of the people, of their language, and of their culture. The tribes were only incidentally involved in business. Unfortunately, our identity as people – our tribal soul – now has an uneasy resting place: That land now owned by our business corporations. If we think that our corporations exist just for corporate purposes, then we have a problem.

Unfortunately our leadership was confronted with and had to deal almost entirely with only one aspect of the problem, and that was the economic aspect. The language of the Settlement Act which our leadership negotiated is dominated by economic considerations. It would be easy to be deceived and think that that's what the Act is all about. We have to realize that economics is only the surface, and that the hope for many other aspects of our culture and our identity are also in the Settlement Act. We have to think about that.

Change

I think that many people don't understand the massive changes that our people had been through and that you people have been through. I think many people forget about the Aleuts and how they barely survived the

Russian invasion. People forget about the changes brought about by the whalers and all their liquor, and by the gold rush, the two World Wars, and by the vast populations that came following the highway and the construction of the railroad. Besides the material changes, there was also a great deal of pressure to conform – to look the same, to speak the same, and to think the same as others do in America.

(Of course we have to understand that the immigrant Americans had their problems, too. They were just a motley collection of people from all over the world trying to make a nation. They had to try to survive – they had to protect themselves – they had to try to get people to think the same way and, of course, they were cultivating and developing and taming the land – just the opposite of what the Indians were trying to do.)

The fact is, Alaska's Native people – just as the Indian people in the "Lower 48" – have fought the same tide of assimilation, acculturation, individualization and atomization. This process has taken its toll on our spirit, on our identity, on our language and on our culture. We have alcoholism and drugs, dropouts, family breakup and crime in our communities because of these pressures we've had on us. We had almost lost the willpower to reassert our tribal identity and reconstitute our languages, which is the expression of our spirit and of who we are, inside.

Rebuilding

We need to rebuild our societies. The education system we have endured has functioned with missionary zeal to break down the bonds that have held us together as a people. Even today, most regions have not found a way to make the school system work to help our children find their identity. Education has been viewed as a panacea – as a cure-all for Native people. But it has also been used by the government, in conjunction with religious groups, as the means of deculturizing our people. Our misled missionaries of education have been drumming into all our people the idea you could not remain an Eskimo or Indian and still be educated. We all know that's a fallacy. It is not true, and we should put to rest the thought that Native people are inherently ignorant. That is a fallacy.

Your great-grandparents and grandparents and parents were the ones that learned the foreign language. Under those circumstances, learning a foreign language was very difficult – a tough mental feat – yet our people learned to communicate in a foreign language, and still do. No thought was given to taking our language of communication and using that as an educational mechanism until recent years; while at the same time, the system was beating our language out of us.

I'm not saying that we should not be educated. Education is essential. It is something that we are participating in – and will continue to participate in – because we require talented professional people at all levels of our enterprises and in our society. But we cannot continue to educate our children at the expense of their identity as Inupiat, Yupik, or Indian, or Aleut people.

Despite all the problems of the past and of the present, we have all the elements for successful future survival. We still have some land (although not all the land we started out with) and we have capital, which is essential in the American economic system. We have some fairly experienced politicians, and we are developing some of the experienced managers that we need.

The Starting Point

I believe that the starting point for dealing with the future has to be a look inward into ourselves. I don't think the main problems that we have are "out there." To me, the real threat for our future survival is inside all of us, individually and tribally.

Our people have been misled to believe that to be an Inupiat or Yupik or Indian or Aleut is incompatible with successful survival in the modern world and that is a fallacy. There is nothing to prevent you from being the best Native person or best linguist and still being a great Alaskan. In fact, if you are Native, you probably could not be a great Alaskan without being great as an Alaskan Native.

Our parents and grandparents were led to believe that if they sent their children three to five thousand miles away, it was going to be good for them. But did they not know that that was the breaking of the spirit of that group of people? Our children were taken not only physically, but spiritually. They could not communicate with their own parents or grandparents any more when they returned home. That was a terribly destructive form of change.

However valuable education may be, it has – and perhaps always will have – the power to destroy us as a people. We cannot look to corporate life or politics to fill the void of a century of psychological repression. Business and politics are not an end. They are simply a means to the primary task of tribal renewal and survival.

More change

The world does not stay still, however, and we must change to survive. Even the billion Chinese decided that they could not wall themselves out from the rest of the world. They had to meet with the ideas and new technology, as well, to survive.

One of the problems that we've had is that we unfortunately divide life into little segments. Some people think the main issue is this housing problem over here, or that it's an alcohol problem over there – or some people think it's the lack of electricity, or another problem somewhere else. But what happens is larger than those little problems. What happens to us as people happens to all of us – not just a part of us. It's not segmented – it's spiritual, it's physical and it's economic.

In my opinion, we have to develop a dynamic program for each of our regional areas that is going to involve, number one, the resurrection of the spirit and of our language and of our culture. That resurrection has to include the creation of an educational system that is not destructive to the spirit and identity of our children. The educational system has to involve economics and corporate life, because we all require dollars to survive nowadays. It also has to involve politics, because it is a political world that we live in. But it must involve the regeneration of our language and culture, because that will give us the basis for the renewal of our people.

AFN

So what I would like to say with reference to the Alaska Federation of Natives, is that I think it has been sort of the target of all our frustrations. Somewhere in our minds, we realize that the economic solutions in the Settlement Act aren't going to solve all our problems even if they succeed economically. We need to realize that AFN is not going to solve all the problems that we have in our own areas.

The AFN has always been primarily political. It was the representation of our unity as we dealt with the outside world. If you question its success, look at its record. The AFN's record speaks for itself.

The Regions

If we are going to move aggressively into the future, it's up to each region and its leaders to control and shape their own destiny. If a region is not doing that, there will be a vast gap that must be filled. We cannot look to the cities for answers. We must look to the regions, because that is where most of our natural leadership is – and that's where our hope is for revitalizing Native identity. That's all I have to say. Thank you.

CHAPTER NOTES

Quotes

Page 12 –   Like 1991 – *Our Stories, Our Lives*, 80
Page 89 –   asking for 40 million – Senate, 8-10 February 1968, 37
Page 94 –   Now my people – Senate, 8-10 February 1968, 288
Page 97 –   The white man – Senate, 12 July 1968, 603
Page 138 –   We are only asking – House 17-18 October 1969, 486
Page 153 –   Most people do not – Senate, 12 July 1968, 406

Prologue

Page 7 –   A little story – Towerak

Introduction

Page 14 –   the only game in town – De Soto, 228
              And yet, in my reading of history – Mallott
              They absolutely control – "Building a Foundation," 4
              Sakuuktugut – Sakuuktugut, 21
Page 15 –   the spirits of our ancestors, Hensley, 1980 AFN keynote
              speech

Chapter 1

Page 17 –   a riveting experience – Shively
              was the son of – Trailblazer
              to the Bureau of Indian Affairs School – Gray
Page 18 –   remarkably advanced – Chase
Page 19 –   A time has come – Gray
Page 20 –   if it wasn't for Nick Gray – Lekanof, Anatoly
Page 21 –   continued on through the 1900s – Fortuine, 199

Chapter 4

Chapter 5

Bibliography, Anagsan

Angasan, Trefon. "Protecting the Subsistence Lifestyle of the Alaska Native People." Rural Development in the Global Perspective 19 December 2002.

"Alaska Natives, The Evolution of Alaska's Subsistence Issue," 2001 Briefing Paper, Alaska Federation of Natives Summit on Subsistence.

"What is Subsistence?" Cultural Survival Quarterly, 2002 Briefing Paper, Alaska Federation of Natives, Summit on Subsistence.

"Alaska Natives, Time Line of Subsistence Policy, May 2002 Alaska Federation of Natives, Board Report

Shadows of the Koyukuk, An Alaskan Native's Life along the River, by Sidney Huntington, Alaska Northwest Books, Anchorage, 1993, page 211

The Great Father in Alaska by Robert E. Price, First Street Press, Douglas, 1990 page 116.

"Alaska Native Claims, Hearings on U.S. 2906," Alaska Federation of Natives Testimony before Committee on Interior and Insular Affairs 90th Congress. Sess.32 (1968)

Briefings and Unofficial Transcript by Alaska Federation of Natives, at U.S. Senate Committee on Indian Affairs Oversight Hearings on Subsistence, April 17, 2002 Subsistence Management Chronology (1925- 2001)

Litigation Update by Heather Kendall, Native American Rights Fund to the Alaska Federation Board of Directors on February 12, 1996.

Subsistence Management Chronology, Alaska Federation of Natives April 17, 2002 to the U.S. Senate Committee on Indian Affairs Oversight Hearings on Subsistence.

Briefings and Unofficial Transcript by Alaska Federation of Natives at U.S. Senate Committee on Indian Affairs Oversight Hearings on Subsistence, April 17, 2002 by Rosita Worl, Ph.D. Sealaska Heritage.

"Building in an Ashen Land," Historical Resource Study of Katmai National Park and Preserve, by Janet Clemens and Frank Norris, National Park Service Alaska Support Office, 1999 Chapter 8, Trapping and Other Subsistence Lifeways.

"Background: Proposal Closure of Upper Naknek River to Gill Net Fishing." By Steven R. Behnke, Technical Paper Number 45, Alaska Department of Fish and Game Division of Subsistence, Dillingham, Alaska December 1, 1981

Congressional Record House August 11, 1994, Report of Committee on Public Bills and Resolutions, by Congressman Don Young.

Alaska Natives and American Laws, Second Edition, David S. Case and David A. Voluck, Fairbanks, Alaska 2002 University of Alaska Fairbanks, Chapter 8 Subsistence in Alaska.

Bibliography, Leggett

D'oro, Rachel. "Explicit Story Lands Teacher in Hot Water." Anchorage Daily News 14 November 1997: A1+

Sullivan, Patty. "Panel Votes Against Book Ban," Anchorage Daily News 3 December 1997: B1+

"State & County Quick Facts,"US Census Bureau. 9-27-2004 <http://quick-facts.census.gov/qfd/states/02000.html>

"Correctional Populations: 2001, Alaska Justice Forum" 9-27-2004 <http://jus-tice.uaa.alaska.edu/forum/f192su02/c_corrpops.html>

Chappell, Ronnie. "Huhndorf Keeping A Stealthy Head, Steady Hands at The Helm of CIRI'S Financial Empire, Leader Steers CIRI On A Wealthy Course Huhndorf Keeps His Eye On Assets – Not Limelight." Anchorage Daily News 23 December 1985: A1+

Works Cited

Books

Ackerman, Robert E. 1975. *The Kenaitze People*. Phoenix: Indian Tribal Series.

Arnold, Robert. 1978. *Alaska Native Land Claims*. Anchorage: The Alaska Native Foundation.

Berger, Thomas R. 1985. *Village Journey: The Report of the Alaska Native Review Commission*. New York: Hill and Wang.

Berry, Mary Clay. 1975. *The Alaska Pipeline, The Politics of Oil and Native Land Claims*. Bloomington & London: Indiana University Press.

Bigjim, Fred, James Ito-Adler. 1974. *Letters to Howard: an Interpretation of the Alaska Native Land Claims*. Anchorage: Alaska Methodist University Press.

Case, David S. 1984. *Alaska Natives and American Laws*. Fairbanks: University of Alaska Press.

Case, David S. 1978. *The Special Relationship of Alaska Natives to the Federal Government: An Historical Analysis*. Anchorage: The Alaska Native Foundation.

Dauenhauer, Nora Marks, Richard Dauenhauer, eds. 1994. *Haa Kusteeyi, Our Culture Tlingit Life Stories*. Juneau, Seattle and London: University of Washington Press, Sealaska Heritage Foundation.

De Soto, Hernando. 2000. *The Mystery of Capital: Why Capitalism Triumphs in the West and Fails Everywhere Else*. New York: Basic Books, A Member of the Perseus Books Group.

Fortuine, Robert. 1986. *Chills and Fever: Health and Disease in the Early History of Alaska*. Anchorage: University of Alaska Press.

Hanrahan, John, Peter Gruenstein. 1977. *Lost Frontier: The Marketing of Alaska*. New York: W.W. Norton & Company, Inc.

Hess, Bill. 1993. Taking Control, The North Slope Borough, The Story of Self Determination in the Arctic. North Slope: North Slope Borough Public Information Division.

Huhndorf, Roy M. 1991. *Reflections on the Alaska Native Experience*. Edited by A.J. McClanahan. Anchorage: The CIRI Foundation.

Kalifornsky, Peter. 1991. *A Dena'ina Legacy, K'tl'eghli Sukdu: The Collected Writings of Peter Kalifornsky*. Edited by Alan Boraas and James Kari. Fairbanks: Alaska Native Language Center UAF.

Kari, James, James A. Fall. 2003. *Shem Pete's Alaska, The Territory of the Upper Cook Inlet Dena'ina*. 2nd Ed. Fairbanks: University of Alaska Press.

Marston, Muktuk. 1972. *Men of the Tundra: Alaska Eskimos at War*. New York: October House, Inc.

McClanahan, Alexandra J. 1986. *Our Stories, Our Lives*. Anchorage: The CIRI Foundation.

McClanahan, Alexandra. 2001. *A Reference in Time*. Anchorage: The CIRI Foundation.

Mitchell, Donald Craig. *Sold American*. New England: UP of New England, 1997.

Morgan, Lael. 1988. *Art and Eskimo Power The Life and Times of Alaskan Howard Rock*. Fairbanks: Epicenter Press.

Naske, Claus-M., Herman E. Slotnick. 1979. *Alaska, A History of the 49th State*. Grand Rapids: William B. Eerdmans Publishing Co.

O'Neill, Dan. 1995. *The Firecracker Boys*. New York: St. Martins' Press.

Price, Robert E. 1990. *The Great Father in Alaska*. Douglas: The First Street Press.

Strickland, Rennard, ed. *Felix S. Cohen's Handbook of Federal Indian Law, 1982 Edition*. 1982. Charlottesville, VA: Michie-Bobbs-Merrill.

▨ Newspapers/Periodicals

Alaska Business Monthly. 2002. "Sealaska Corp., Hard times have fallen on this Native corporation, but there is hope for a brighter future." Vol. 18: 3. March 2002, 73.

Alaska Native Management Report. 1973. "Regions Asked to Establish Ground Rules for Resource Revenue Sharing." Vol. 2: 11. 12 June 1973, 12.

Alaska Native Management Report. 1973. "Financial Analysis of Act Completed." Vol. 2: 19. 18 October 1973, 4-5/7.

Alaska Native Management Report. 1974. "NANA, SOCAL Agree to Drill Exploratory Wells." Vol. 3: 17. 30 September 1974, 3.

Alaska Native Management Report. 1976. "Oversight hearings: Congressional intent flouted, say Native leaders." Vol. 5: 11. 15 June 1976, 1/8.

Alaska Native Management Report. 1976. "NANA Splits $2 million in 7(i) Funds." Vol. 5: 20. 1 November, 1976, 1/6.

Arnott, Sarah. 1981. "The Alaska Native Claims Settlement Act: Legislation Appropriate to the Past and the Future." American Indian Law Review. Vol. 9, 135.

Black, Kathryn A., David H. Bundy, Cynthia Pickering Christianson, Cabot Christianson. 1989. "When Worlds Collide: Alaska Native Corporations and the Bankruptcy Code." Alaska Law Review, Vol. 6:73.

Goodman, Richard. 1973. "Charitable Donations Under the Alaska Native Claims Settlement Act." UCLA Alaska Law Review, Vol. 3:148.

Juneau Empire. 1999. "Between Worlds, How the Alaska Native Claims Settlement Act Reshaped the Destinies of Alaska's Native People." A Juneau Empire Special Report.

Lazarus, Arthus, Sr. W. Richard West, Sr. 1976. "The Alaska Native Claims Settlement Act: A Flawed Victory," Law and Contemporary Problems. Vol. 40, No. 1 Winter 1976.

Linxwiler, James D. 1992. "The Alaska Native Claims Settlement Act: The First 20 years." 38 Rocky Mineral Law Institute. 2-1(59).

McClanahan, Alexandra J. "In 1966: It Took Money, an Organization and a Paper," CIRI Shareholder Update, Vol. 23, No. 9, November/December 1998, 4/7.

Moster, Todd. 1981. "The Effects of Increased Tribal and State Autonomy on the Special Relationship Between Alaska Natives and the Federal Government: An Overview." UCLA Alaska Law Review. Vol 10: 183.

Trailblazer. 1965. "Personality of the Month, Nick Gray," Cook Inlet Native Association.

Walsh, John F. 1985. "Settling the Alaska Native Claims Settlement Act." Stanford Law Review, November. Vol. 38:227.

Work, Shannon D. 1987. "Alaska Native Claims Settlement Act." Oregon Law Review Vol. 66, 1987.

Articles/Records/Personal Records

Alaska Federation of Natives. 1971. AFN Report on Alaska Native Land Claims Status. Anchorage: Alaska Federation of Natives.

Alaska Federation of Natives. 1989. "The AFN Report on the Status of Alaska Natives: A Call for Action." Anchorage: Alaska Federation of Natives.

Alaska Federation of Natives. 1988. "1991: Making It Work, A Guide to Public

Law 100-241 1987 Amendments to the Alaska Native Claims Settlement Act." Anchorage: Alaska Federation of Natives.

Alaska Native Policy Center. 2004. "Our Choices, Our Future, Analysis of the Status of Alaska Natives Report 2004." Anchorage: Alaska Native Policy Center. July.

Alexander Creek Inc. 2000. "Alexander Creek, These Voices Should be Heard." Anchorage: Alexander Creek Inc., 22 May.

ANCSA Research: Abstracts & Articles. 1996. Unpublished binders Blythe Marston, ed.

Arctic Slope Regional Corporation. 2002. Unpublished, "Regional Corporation Section 7(i) Distribution History." November.

Case, David S. 1995. "In a Twinkling – The Alaska Native Claims Settlement Act & Agreements Relating to the Use and Development of Land." Prepared for Indigenous Land Use Agreements Conference, September 26-28, Darwin, Northern Territory, Australia.

Gray, Nick. 1966. "Nick Gray's Speech." State Wide Native Conference, 19 October.

Groh, Clifford John. 1976. "Oil, Money, Land and Power: The Passage of the Alaska Native Claims Settlement Act of 1971." diss., Harvard Kennedy School of Politics.

Hensley, William L. 1966. "What Rights to Land Have the Alaskan Natives?" University of Alaska Constitutional Law, 17 May.

Hensley, William L. 1980. "The Land is the Spirit of the People," Alaska Federation of Natives Keynote Speech, 23 October.

Honeycutt, Jackie. 2002. Unpublished 7(i) data. December.

Marrs, Carl H. 2003. "ANCSA: An Act of Self-Determination, Harnessing Business Endeavors to Achieve Alaska Native Goals." Cultural Survival Quarterly. Cambridge: Cultural Survival. Vol. 27:3, 28-30.

McClanahan, Alexandra J., Jangila D. Hillas. 2001. "Building a Foundation for Alaska's Economic Destiny," ANCSA Regional Corporation Presidents/CEOs, 1-16.

McClanahan, Alexandra J., Julee Duhrsen. 2002. "Native Corporations: An Epic Story Benefiting Alaska," ANCSA Regional Corporation Presidents/CEOs, 1-16.

McClanahan, Alexandra J., Julee Duhrsen. 2003. "Native Corporations: A Legacy of Sharing," ANCSA Regional Corporation Presidents/CEOs, 1-14.

McClanahan, Alexandra J., Cindy Allred, Rolf Dagg. 2004. "Sakuuktugut: We are working incredibly hard," A look at selected data for 13 Regional Corporations and 30 village corporations, ANCSA Regional Corporation Presidents/CEOs, 1-21.

McClanahan, Alexandra J., Cindy Allred, Rof Dagg. 2005. "Mulrugni Yuuluni: Walking In Two Worlds With One Spirit, A look at selected data for 13 Native Regional Corporations and 28 Native Village Corporations," ANCSA Regional Corporation Presidents/CEOs, 1-22.

Otte,Vicki. 7 (i) presentation, December 2005.

Paul, Frederick. Then Fight For It! Alaska Historical Commission Studies in History. 10 June.

Peratrovich, betsy, personal papers.

Price, Monroe E. 1979. "A Moment in History: The Alaska Native Claims Settlement Act." UCLA-Alaska Law Review. Vol. 8: 89.

Silko, Leslie Marmon. 1996. "Landscape, History, and the Pueblo Imagination," The Nature Reader. Edited by Daniel Halpern and Dan Frank. New Jersey: Ecco Press.

Stein, Gary C. 1976. "Uprooted Native Casualties of the Aleutian Campaign of World War II." Fairbanks: University of Alaska Fairbanks.

Van Ness, Feldman, Sutcliffe, Curtis & Levenberg. 1981. RE: Issues Confronting the Alaska Native People—Memorandum. Washington, D.C.: A Professional Corporation.

Wolfe, Robert J. 1982. "Alaska's Great Sickness, 1900: Measles and Influenza in a Virgin Soil Population." Proceedings of the American Philosophical Society.

Government Records

44: Federal-State Land Use Planning Commission for Alaska. Alaska Native Claims Settlement Act 1971-1979. 1979. Joint Federal-State Land Use Planning Commission for Alaska.

Alaska Natives Commission. 1994. Final Report, Volume 1. Anchorage: Joint Federal-State Commission on Policies and Program Affecting Alaska Natives.

American Indian Policy Review Commission. 1976. "Special Joint Task Force Report on Alaskan Native Issues." Washington: U.S. Government Printing Office.

Federal Field Committee for Development Planning in Alaska. 1968. Alaska
     Natives and the Land. Anchorage, Washington, D.C.: U.S. Government
     Printing Office.
Jones, Richard S. 1972. "Alaska Native Claims Settlement Act of 1971 (Public
     Law 92-203): History and Analysis." Congressional Research Service,
     Library of Congress.
Price, Robert E. 1982, Native Rights, Legal Status of the Alaska Natives, A
     Report to the Alaska Statehood Commission. Department of Law, State of
     Alaska.
Price, Robert E. 1984. Alaska Native Claims Settlement Act (ANCSA) ANCSA
     1985 Study June 29, 1984 Draft. Anchorage: United States Department of
     the Interior, 29 June.
Public Law 92-203. 1971. 92nd Congress.
U.S. House Committee on Interior and Insular Affairs. 1969. Hearings before
     the Subcommittee on Indian Affairs, H.R. 13142 and H.R. 10193, 91st
     Congress, 1st sess., 4,5,6 August and 9 September.
U.S. House Committee on Interior and Insular Affairs. 1969. Hearings before
     the Subcommittee on Indian Affairs, H.R. 13142, H.R. 10193 and H.R.
     14212, 91st Congress, 1st sess., 17, 18 October.
U.S. Senate. 1971. Alaska Native Claims Settlement Act of 1971, Report
     together with Additional and Supplemental Views.
U.S. Senate Committee on Interior and Insular Affairs. 1968. Hearings on
     Alaska Native Land Claims, S. 1964, S. 2690, S. 2020 and S. 3586, 90th
     Congress, 2nd sess., 12 July.
U.S. Senate Committee on Interior and Insular Affairs. 1968. Hearings on
     Alaska Native Land Claims, S. 2906, S. 1964, S. 2690, S. 2020, 90th
     Congress, 2nd sess., 8-10 February.
U.S. Senate Committee on Interior and Insular Affairs. 1969. Hearings on
     Alaska Native Land Claims, S. 1830, 91st Congress, 1st sess., 7-8 August,
     534.
U.S. Senate Committee on Interior and Insular Affairs. 1971. Hearings on
     Alaska Native Land Claims, S. 35, S. 835, and S. 1571, 92nd Congress,
     1st sess., 29 August.
U.S. Senate Committee on Interior and Insular Affairs. 1976. Oversight of the
     Implementation of the Alaska Natives Claims Settlement Act, 94th
     Congress, 2nd sess., 10 & 14 June.

Interviews by author

Adams, Jake, interviews, winter 2002.
Angasan, Trefon, tape recording, 28 July 1998.
Boyko, Edgar Paul, tape recording, 7 May 1999.
Brown, Margie, telephone interview, winter 2001.
Case, David, interview, October 2001.
Chase, Sophie, tape recording, 5 April 1999.
Eaton, Hank, tape recording, 13 April 1999.
Hawkins, Tom, telephone interview, October 2002.
Haycox, Stephen, interview, winter 2001.
Huhndorf, Roy, tape recording, 24 November 1998 and 2 and 31 May 2000.
Irvin, George, telephone interview, winter 2001.
Kito, Sam, tape recording, May 1992.
Kroloff, Mark, interview, winter 2001.
Leavitt, Oliver, interviews, winter 2002.
Lekanof, Anatoly, tape recording, 9 February, 1999.
Lekanof, Flore Sr., tape recording, 19 January 1999.
Mallott, Byron, tape recording, 23 July 1998 and 30 November 1998, CIRI, Anchorage; telephone interview, winter 2002.
Marrs, Carl, interviews, winter 2002.
Martin, Stella, tape recording, 22 April 1999.
Mery, Jim, telephone interview, winter 2002.
Nelson, Judy, telephone interview, October 2002.
Potts, Karl, interviews, October-December 2002.
Shively, John, tape recording, 17 December 1998; various interviews, 2002.
Towarak, Tim, email, 21 September 1998.
Uhl, Bob and Carrie, tape recording, 9 July 1999.

Seminar

Van Ness, Bill. 2002. UAA Alaska Native Studies, ANCSA Revisited, Seminar Four, "Formation of the Different Corporations." 20 April, Anchorage.

Other

Inter-Office Memorandum to Roy M. Huhndorf, George V. Kriste, Operating Committee from Stephen C. Hillard, Vice President and General Counsel. 1988. CIRI's Section 7(i) Management Priorities in Light of Sealaska Actions, Nov. 28.

Report of the Special Master pursuant to Fed. R. Civ. P.53. 1983. U.S. District Court for the District of Alaska, The Aleut Corporation et al. V. Arctic Slope Regional Corporation, et al., Ralph Wienshienk, 28 March.

Section 7(i) Settlement Agreement. 1982. 29 June.

Internet:

Ahtna Inc.
"About Ahtna Inc."   February 24, 2004
www.ahtna-Inc.com/about_ahtna.html

Aleut
"Aleutian East Borough" Community Overview February 24, 2004
www.dced.state.ak.us/dca/commdb/CF_BLOCK.htm
"Ecological sub regions of the United States" Chapter 7. February 24, 2004
www.fs.fed.us/land/pubs/ecoregions/ch7.html

ASRC
"Northslope Borough homepage" February 26, 2004
www.co.north-slope.ak.us/nsb/default.htm
"Northslope Borough" Community Overview February 26, 2004
www.dced.state.ak.us/dca/commdb/CF_BLOCK.htm

Bering Straits
"General Information" Nome Convention and Visitors Bureau February 27, 2004
www.nomealaska.org/vc/information.htm

Bristol Bay
"Bristol Bay Borough" Community Overview February 26, 2004
www.dced.state.ak.us/dca/commdb/CF_BLOCK.htm

Calista
"Bethel" Community Overview February 26, 2004
www.dced.state.ak.us/dca/commdb/CF_BLOCK.htm
"Land and Natural Resources" February 26, 2004
www.calistacorp.com/resdev.html
"General Overview" February 26,2004
www.calistacorp.com/profile.html

Chugach Alaska
"The Lands Department" February 26,2004
www.chugach-ak.com/landsmain.html

Doyon
"Fairbanks" Community Overview February 26, 2004
www.dced.state.ak.us/dca/commdb/CF_BLOCK.htm

Kodiak
"Kodiak Island Geography" February 27, 2004
www.kodiak.org/geography.html

NANA
"Nana History" February 27, 2004
www.nana.com/history.htm

Sealaska
"Explore Southeast" " February 27, 2004
www.travelalaska.com/regions/regionhome.aspx?regionid=20&pagetitle=inside
    %20passage

ACKNOWLEDGEMENTS _____

Many people made this book possible, so many, in fact, it's humbling to realize how much help they gave me – and so graciously. On these pages I wish to acknowledge many of them for their assistance and support. These people and others, too, deserve the credit for what is good and useful about this book, and I take full responsibility for any mistakes and omissions in the text.

The person most responsible for this book's existence is Carl Marrs, former CIRI president and CEO, who hired me in 1998 to begin the process of documenting the history of the Alaska Native Claims Settlement Act. Carl gave me the privilege and honor of learning as much as possible about ANCSA, and his guidance and support have changed my life. I am also grateful to Margie Brown, Carl's successor, who has allowed me to continue my work at CIRI. I am also grateful to my mother, Jeanne McClanahan. She is my hero because she had the courage to take great risks, which led to tragic failures and great successes. She died on May 2, 2004, at age 85 years.

Aaron Leggett, who has been working with me faithfully for the last three years, deserves so much credit for all his work, not to mention his patience for all the times I started down the path of wondering how we could ever complete this task. In addition to writing his chapter and assisting on all phases of this book, Aaron deserves special mention for working with each of the regions to develop the regional biographies, and he also worked hard to gather photographs and obtain permissions for their use. My advisor at Alaska Pacific University, Dr. Timothy Rawson, played a pivotal role in encouraging me, but always in a quiet, unassuming manner seemingly aimed at getting me to think the idea was mine and not his. Without his gentle guidance and many valuable suggestions, this work would not exist. Playing similar roles on a smaller scale were Dr. Mei Mei Evans and Dr. Doug North of APU.

My friend Hazel Felton of CIRI has found ways to inspire and encourage my spiritual growth, and I owe her much gratitude for teaching me the importance of speaking from your heart and honoring your mother.

A former supervisor, Bill Schoephoester, deserves special mention, because it was he who loaned me his copy of Hernando de Soto's *The Mystery of Capital.* As a result of de Soto's book, my eyes were opened to the new form of capitalism being created by Alaska Native Corporations. I also thank Sheri

Buretta, who has provided me with excellent suggestions on revisions to this work, as well as much needed support.

Susan A. Anderson, president and CEO of The CIRI Foundation, gave me a deadline for completing this book, and without her nudging as well as her tireless support, I would probably still be thinking about what to write. The entire staff of the Anchorage Museum of History and Art inspired me greatly by supporting the work I did with Opal Sidon on the permanent ANCSA exhibit in the Alaska Gallery, especially Marilyn Knapp and Dave Nicholls. The exhibit forced us to explain this complex act in a small space. Opal, who worked with me for several months as a result of generous support by Marie Ireland and Tony Delia at the Arctic Slope Regional Corporation, kept me on task during my mother's illness and death. As a result, I will always have a special place in my heart for Opal.

Stephen Haycox, my collaborator on the "Alaska History Scrapbook," printed weekly in the Anchorage Daily News and history professor at the University of Alaska Anchorage, has quietly cheered me on and guided and encouraged me over the last seven years. I am also grateful to the Anchorage Daily News for its support for the "Alaska History Scrapbook, and especially to our patient editor at the newspaper Frank Gerjevic and his former supervisor Steve Lindbeck.

My supervisors during my tenure at CIRI have been inspiring and have always encouraged me, beginning with Barbara Donatelli, and including Sophie Minich and Pam Allen. I am currently employed by Cook Inlet Tribal Council, and I owe so much to Gloria O'Neill for being the shining star that she is.

My example in the development of this book has been Robert Arnold's classic *Alaska Native Land Claims*. As a matter of fact, I view *Sakuuktugut* as an updated version of Bob's book. Several years before his death, Bob suggested we collaborate on such a project. We never pulled all the pieces together, but Bob set me on the right path with his suggestion. I also owe a great deal to Lydia Hays, who worked with Bob on his book and has worn many important hats throughout the years.

Allison Knox has encouraged me by cheering me on and providing tremendous support for all of my efforts in her entirely unselfish, gracious and selfless manner.

Mark Kroloff, former Chief Operating Officer of CIRI, assisted me in many ways, but most importantly by always urging me to try harder, reach higher and do a better job. Mark never settles for "good enough" whenever it is possible to reach for the best.

Tina Wallace deserves special thanks for taking on the huge task of designing this work on her own free time and as an unpaid volunteer. Her example sets a high bar indeed for volunteers.

Many Alaska Native leaders gave me the gift of their time and wisdom and graciously submitted to hours and hours of oral history interviews. I owe special thanks to Byron Mallott, Willie Hensley, Roy Huhndorf, Don Wright, Anatoly Lekanof, Bob and Carrie Uhl, Sophie Prosser and many others.

Ruth Sampson gave us the gift of her knowledge of the Inupiaq language to help us arrive at the title, *Sakuuktugut*. I am grateful to Bradley Bodfish, an intern from the Arctic Slope Regional Corporation, who helped me select the word "sakuuktugut" and who also worked with me on one of our economic impact reports. Jim Kilpatrick, who farms my land in Nebraska, has taught me so much about stewardship and putting one's heart into efforts to take care of the land – because it's the right thing to do.

Among many others who deserve my thanks are Rob Stapleton, David Swenson, Blake Kowal, Chris Arend, Ukpeagvik Inupiat Corp., Bill Hess, Hallie Bissett, Debra Bissett, Bill Van Ness, John Shively, Vicki Otte, Jangila Hilas, Cindy Allred, Kathy Porterfield, Trefon Angasan, Chief Gary Harrison, betsy Peratrovich, the Association of ANCSA Presidents/CEOs, Alan Boraas, Pat Wolf, Kathleen Hertel, and poets Joan Hoffman and Annette Penniman.